Leader's / Catech

Catholicism

and

Reason

Rev. Edward J. Hayes
Rev. Msgr. Paul J. Hayes
and James J. Drummey

C.R. Publications Inc.
345 Prospect Street
Norwood, Massachusetts 02062

NIHIL OBSTAT
Msgr. William E. Maguire
Censor Librorum

IMPRIMATUR
Most Rev. John C. Reiss
Bishop of Trenton
August 28, 1996

The Nihil Obstat and Imprimatur are official declarations that a book or pamphlet is free of doctrinal or moral error. No implication is contained therein that those who have granted the Nihil Obstat or Imprimatur agree with the contents, opinions, or statements expressed.

Cover design by Jeff Giniewicz
Printed in the United States of America

ISBN 0-9649087-2-7

Contents

How to Get the Most Out of This Book

The purpose of *Catholicism and Reason* is to present in popular language the fundamental structure and reasons underlying Catholicism and to explain the principal beliefs of Catholics. Because it reaffirms the basic convictions by which Catholics should live, *Catholicism and Reason* will appeal to a wide audience—from high school students to senior citizens. It is an excellent text for adults, whether in formal courses, informal study groups, or RCIA classes; for college and university students; and for those in Catholic high schools or parish religious education programs.

The book is a valuable tool because it offers not only a full-year study of the foundations of Catholicism, but it can also be broken down into mini-courses. Some examples:

1. A fourteen-hour Apologetics course on how to find Christ's Church in the world today (chapters 1-14).

2. An eight-hour course on the Apostles' Creed and the role of the Blessed Mother in the Church (chapters 15-22).

3. A four-hour course on Jesus Christ (chapters 5-8).

4. A four-hour course on the Church (chapters 9-12).

There are other possibilities and variations as well, depending on what beliefs need to be stressed or what religious voids need to be filled. For example, we have given a six-week course on chapters 1-12 during Lent— one night a week, two hours a night, with a coffee break between classes. Or you could give a four-hour course on our Lord in one day—covering the humanity and divinity of Jesus in the morning and his Passion and Resurrection in the afternoon—with a break for lunch and a Mass celebrated at the conclusion of the program.

But whatever material and format you choose, few books lend themselves better to an organized and systematic presentation of the Catholic Faith than *Catholicism and Reason*. The text will accomplish a goal stated by Pope John Paul II in his apostolic exhortation *On Catechesis in Our Time*, that is, to help prepare Catholics "to make a defense to anyone who calls them to account for the hope that is in them" (n. 25).

Catholicism and Reason also lends itself easily to discussion. Specific suggestions for stimulating interest and initiating discussion can be found under the individual chapters. These suggestions, of course, are not all-encompassing, but they should provide some practical ideas for the catechist or group leader.

The chapters contain more than sufficient information for classes of forty-five to sixty minutes. How this time is divided between lecture and discussion depends on the teacher and the students. Some groups are more responsive than others and make the catechist's job easier. Whatever the situation, no catechist should have difficulty preparing an interesting and effective class.

Generally speaking, the suggestions for presenting the material will be helpful whether you are teaching high schoolers or adults, although there are certain topics, questions, and projects that will be more appropriate for one age group than another. The instructor will have to be the judge of that.

In addition to the specific tips on teaching from *Catholicism and Reason*, the following general comments, not necessarily in the order of their importance, may be helpful.

1. *Read the entire book and catechist's manual before you begin teaching.* Not only should you do this to familiarize yourself with the entire course, but you will find material in the latter section of the book that may be useful in presenting the earlier chapters. For example, chapter 16 in the book and the manual should be read in conjunction with chapter 2; and chapter 14 in conjunction with chapter 3. Familiarity with the entire book will also be helpful if you are questioned about a matter that is covered later in the course. You could then answer the question briefly, note that it will be taken up in more detail at another time, and refer the questioner to the appropriate chapter for additional information.

2. *Although the material in* Catholicism and Reason *can be presented effectively in lecture form, the ideal way to de-*

velop it is through discussion. Students are more likely to remember things if they have had a chance to talk about them, ask questions, and even reason to some of the answers themselves. By discussion, it should be made clear, we do not mean an aimless stream of consciousness where everybody's opinion is equally valid and where nothing is resolved. We mean rather an atmosphere where the teacher teaches and the student learns; where questions, comments, and dialogue are encouraged under the guidance and direction of the instructor; where facts are stated by the catechist if the students do not come up with them; and where the teacher summarizes the matter discussed at the end of the class, answering all questions as well as possible and trying to resolve all doubts.

3. *Instead of merely stating the points to be covered, teachers should seek to draw the information out of the students.* Catechists should be constantly asking questions, making the students think, and inviting them to participate in the class. When you first ask a question, do not direct it to a particular student lest the others in the class assume that they are safe and can stop paying attention. Ask the question first of the entire class and then, if no one volunteers an answer, direct it to a particular person. Do not allow a few students to monopolize the discussion. Try to involve everyone, especially those who seem not to be paying attention. Be careful not to embarrass the shy or reticent student, but try to bring him or her out of their shell. When students ask what you think about some matter, turn the question back to them and ask, "What do you think?" Your goal is to keep all the students involved in the class.

4. *Keep the class interesting and current through the use of stories, anecdotes, and up-to-date items related to the subject matter.* Storytelling is an effective way to make a point, as our Lord proved with his use of parables. Teachers must know the Gospels and can weave stories around the events in the life of Jesus with the assistance of a life of Christ or a biblical commentary. Have the students bring into class pertinent items from newspapers and magazines. Get them in the habit of watching for new papal statements or Church pronouncements, developments in the field of ecumenism, or ex-

amples of the effects of original sin on the world, and you will have a successful class. Remember, however, that media accounts of religious issues are often slanted, out of context, misleading, or just plain wrong. Insist that authentic documents, not some reporter's biased view of a Church teaching, be used to form the basis of any valid discussion.

5. *Define all terms, even if it seems unnecessary.* You should not assume that any religious term is understood correctly, so ask the students what it means and then spell out the definition for them. A Catholic dictionary or encyclopedia, or the glossary section of the *Catholic Almanac*, will be most helpful in providing definitions. Unless the students understand exactly what you are talking about, you will either lose them or misinform them. A good secular dictionary, even though not Catholic, can also provide accurate definitions of religious terms.

And don't be afraid to have the students memorize some of these definitions. As Pope John Paul has said, "A certain memorization of the words of Jesus, of important Bible passages, of the Ten Commandments, of the formulas of profession of the faith, of the liturgical texts, of the essential prayers, of key doctrinal ideas, etc., far from being opposed to the dignity of young Christians, or constituting an obstacle to personal dialogue with the Lord, is a real need. . . . We must be realists. The blossoms, if we may call them that, of faith and piety do not grow in the desert places of a memory-less catechesis" (*On Catechesis in Our Time*, n. 55).

6. *Use the chalkboard and other visual aids as much as possible.* The old saying that one picture is worth a thousand words is still true. The material on the Passion in chapter 7 is very powerful as a story; it can be even more powerful when supplemented by a crown of thorns, a scourge, a crosspiece similar to what Jesus carried, and some railroad spikes. Any maps, films, slides, pictures, etc., that can be used to illustrate a point will add immeasurably to your class. Simply writing things on the board will also make a difference in getting the material across to the students. Do not neglect any tool, particularly videos and games (Hangman, Jeopardy, etc.) that will make your class more informative and interesting.

7. *Review what you have covered previously.* Since the first fourteen chapters are a logical, step-by-step summary of how to find the Church of Christ today, you should at the beginning of each class summarize, or have the students summarize, what has been established thus far. In this way, the total picture will always be clear. If time permits, you could give brief quizzes at the beginning of class to prepare the ground for the next phase of the course. Quizzes and tests are important, even in once-a-week religious education classes, if we expect the students to take the subject seriously.

8. *State the position of the Church clearly and unequivocally.* Your job is not to give your own opinion or that of some popular theologian, but rather the definitive teaching of the infallible Church of Christ. "Catechists for their part," Pope John Paul said, "must have the wisdom to pick from the field of theological research those points that can provide light for their own reflection and their teaching, drawing, like the theologians, from the true sources, in the light of the magisterium. They must refuse to trouble the minds of the children and young people, at this stage of their catechesis, with outlandish theories, useless questions, and unproductive discussions, things that St. Paul often condemned in his pastoral letters" (*On Catechesis in Our Time,* n. 61).

This adherence to the truth is a solemn responsibility. Make sure that the class always knows what the Church's teaching is and the reason for that teaching. If you do not know the answer to a question, do not try to fool the students. Tell them that you will find the answer—and then do so. Do not get bogged down in certain areas, and do not worry if you cannot completely convince all your students about the merits of a specific teaching. Do your best to present the view of the Church and then leave it to the Holy Spirit to enlighten the minds of your listeners. When discussing other religions, do not water down Catholic beliefs. But at the same time, do not belittle others for their beliefs. You can disagree with other religions while still showing charity towards those who belong to them.

9. *Assign projects and homework so as to involve the class more deeply in the course.* This course offers a unique opportunity to encourage familiarity with sacred Scripture and es-

pecially the Gospels. There are also reference works that the students could use for reports to the class. Have one or two students give a five-minute talk each class. This will prepare them to talk about Christ and the Church just as freely and intelligently as they talk about sports or politics. Speaking of references, there are certain books that are invaluable to teachers and should be a part of their own library. These books include a Bible, a Catholic dictionary, a one-volume Catholic encyclopedia, a Catholic almanac, the *Catechism of the Catholic Church*, a life of Christ, a dictionary of the saints, and a good question-and-answer book, such as *Catholic Replies*.

10. *Encourage daily prayer and frequent reception of the Sacraments.* Take advantage of the numerous reminders throughout the course to mention the necessity of daily prayer, at least weekly Mass and Communion, and at least monthly Confession. Begin and end each class with a prayer, inviting the students to suggest prayers and to lead the class in saying them. A decade of the rosary is a good way to start a class period. The catechist can be an actual grace for the students by inspiring them to do good and avoid evil and always to remain close to Jesus and his Church. Teachers who demonstrate a sincere interest in the well-being of their students, who pray with them and for them, who are available to them after class for any help or advice they may need can have a positive and long-lasting influence on the young people entrusted to them.

Effective catechesis depends upon "the faith, hope, and love of catechists, responding to God's grace by growing in these virtues and ministering to others," said the U.S. Bishops in the concluding paragraph of *Sharing the Light of Faith.* "The person of the catechist is the medium in which the message of the Faith is incarnated. Whether catechists be parents, teachers, religious, priests, bishops, or any other of God's people, their witness to faith plays a pivotal role in catechesis."

11. *For high school religion teachers, acquaint the parents of your students with the course.* There are three things necessary for a successful program—good books, good teachers, and interested parents. We have **provided** the first requirement and contributed to the se**cond**. The third is up to

you. Contact all the parents at the beginning of the religious education year, explain the course to them (you could send them a photocopy of the "The Chain of Faith" on pages 159-161), urge them to send their children to class faithfully, and invite them to visit the classroom or to contact you if they have any questions or suggestions. Some students will tell parents that they don't want to go to class because "we're not learning anything." Parents who know what is being taught to their children will not be swayed by that argument.

12. *It is important for the teacher to realize that the work of helping others to grow and mature in the Christian life is primarily the work of the Holy Spirit.* The catechist, Pope John Paul said, "must be very much aware of acting as a living, pliant instrument of the Holy Spirit. To invoke this Spirit constantly, to be in communion with him, to endeavor to know his authentic inspirations must be the attitude of the teaching Church and of every catechist" (*On Catechesis in Our Time,* n. 72).

"The fundamental tasks of catechists," the Bishops of the United States said in *Sharing the Light of Faith,* "are to proclaim Christ's message, to participate in efforts to develop community, to lead people to worship and prayer, and to motivate them to serve others" (n. 213). In order to be effective teachers, the Bishops said, catechists "must have a solid grasp of Catholic doctrine and worship, familiarity with Scripture, communications skills, the ability to use various methodologies, understanding of how people grow and mature, and of how persons of different ages and circumstances learn" (n. 211).

But perhaps most important, the Bishops said, "the catechist must be fully committed to Jesus Christ. Faith must be shared with conviction, joy, love, enthusiasm, and hope. . . . To give witness to the gospel, the catechist must establish a living, ever-deepening relationship with the Lord. He or she must be a person of prayer, one who frequently reflects on the Scriptures and whose Christlike living testifies to deep faith. Only men and women of faith can share faith with others, preparing the setting within which people can respond in faith to God's grace" (n. 207).

Chapter 1

Grasping for the Truth

Purpose: The purpose of this chapter is to introduce the course to the students, to make it seem interesting and appealing to them. A secondary purpose, since this is the first class, is to set down certain rules covering conduct in class for the remainder of the year.

Tips for Teachers: The first part of this class will necessarily have to be taken up with seating arrangements, attendance, and rules for classroom conduct. It will be important for the teacher of high school students to state clearly what is expected of the teenagers. The atmosphere created in the first class can set the tone for the year. Catechists should express their policies and expectations to the students clearly and firmly so as to prevent misunderstandings and problems from arising later on. One obvious and essential rule is that only one person speaks at a time, either the teacher or one of the students who has been properly recognized. A courteous and respectful atmosphere is the only setting in which religion or any other subject can be effectively presented by the catechist and completely understood by the students.

The teacher should also mention such things as homework assignments, quizzes, tests, and special projects—in other words, the various techniques and methods that will be used to develop the subject matter, impart knowledge to the students, and encourage them to practice their Faith.

Once the preliminaries are over, the remainder of the class should be spent discussing the general nature and purpose of the course, with emphasis on some of the more interesting and challenging subjects to be covered—the existence of God, the miracles of Christ and those occurring in modern times, the medical and historical analysis of the Passion of Christ, the historical evidence for the resurrection, papal infallibility, ecumenism, heaven, hell, purgatory, and the role of the Blessed Mother in the Church and in the world. The teacher may introduce any of these subjects or use the discussion topics and questions which follow.

Topics for Discussion:

1. Does religion play an important part in people's lives today?

2. Give some examples of an interest in God and religion today.

3. Give some examples of people who seem to keep religious principles far removed from their daily activities.

4. Does separation of church and state mean that God has no place in the workings of government?

5. What do you want to learn from this course?

Some Questions and Answers:

1. What was the Second Vatican Council and what did it accomplish?

A. The Second Vatican Council, which was convened on October 11, 1962 by Pope John XXIII, brought together in Rome more than 2,500 Catholic bishops from all parts of the world to discuss ways of presenting the eternal teachings of Christ to the modern world, and also to foster among all Christians that unity which Jesus has with his Father.

During its four sessions, which concluded on December 8, 1965, the Council Fathers promulated sixteen documents— two dogmatic constitutions (on the Church and on Divine Revelation), two pastoral constitutions (on the Sacred Liturgy and on the Church in the Modern World), three declarations (on Christian Education, on Religious Freedom, and on the Relationship of the Church to Non-Christian Religions), and nine decrees (on the Bishops' Pastoral Office in the Church, on Priestly Formation, on the Appropriate Renewal of the Religious Life, on the Ministry and Life of Priests, on the Apostolate of the Laity, on the Church's Missionary Activity, on Ecumenism, on Eastern Catholic Churches, and on the Instruments of Social Communication).

2. What are the two most fundamental religious principles?
A. Love God and love your neighbor. To love God means to worship him, to keep his Commandments, to thank him for the blessings he has bestowed on us. To love our neighbor means to treat him or her as you would have them treat you, to help others when they are in need.

Projects:

1. Summarize one of the documents of Vatican II.
2. Write a short biographical sketch of your local bishop.
3. Write a short paper on one teaching of the Church that you strongly agree with and give your reasons.
4. Write a short paper on one teaching of the Church that you strongly disagree with and give your reasons.

References:

Catechism of the Catholic Church
Catholic Almanac
Drummey, James J. Catholic Replies
Duggan, G. H. Beyond Reasonable Doubt
Encyclopedia of Catholic History. Edited by Matthew
      Bunson
Flannery, Austin. Vatican Council II: The Conciliar and
      Post-Conciliar Documents (2 vols.)
Hardon, John. The Catholic Catechism
_____. Modern Catholic Dictionary
_____. The Question and Answer Catholic Catechism
Keating, Karl. What Catholics Believe
Kreeft, Peter. Fundamentals of the Faith
_____. and Tacelli, Ronald K. Handbook of Christian
      Apologetics
Most, William. Catholic Apologetics Today
Nevins, Albert J., M.M., Catholicism: The Faith of Our
      Fathers
Sheed, Frank. Theology for Beginners
Wuerl, Donald, Lawler, Thomas and Lawler, Ronald. The
      Catholic Catechism
_____. The Teaching of Christ

Chapter 2

The Search for God

Purpose: The purpose of this chapter is to show several ways of reasoning to the existence of God.

Tips for Teachers: Begin the class by writing the word "God" on the board and asking the students for whatever words this suggests to them. As the words are called out, write them on the board in three separate columns— those related to God the Father, those related to Jesus, and those related to the Church. There will be some overlapping—words that could go under more than one heading—but generally the columns might look something like this:

God	*Jesus Christ*	*Church*
Creator	Savior	People of God
Father	Redeemer	Saints
Old Testament	Sacraments	Pope
Ten Commandments	Passion	Bishops
Prophets	Resurrection	Mass
Religion	New Testament	Miracles

Do not put the headings above each column until you have listed all the words. Then, as you identify each column, explain that the course will cover these three all-important realities—God, Jesus, and the Church—and that in this particular class you will discuss God and whether we can use our reason to show that he really exists.

The remainder of the class should be used to explain the three proofs for the existence of God—historical, uncaused cause, and intelligent design—either by having the catechist outline them or, preferably, by drawing them out of the students through the use of the topics and questions listed below. Teachers are encouraged to use the many examples for each proof that ap-

16

pear in the chapter, but you should be constantly on the lookout for more current items to support your case. The more outside material that you or your students can bring into class, the more interesting and enjoyable the class will be.

The question of evolution will usually arise or, if not, the teacher should bring it up so that it may be properly defined and the position of the Church may be stated. Do not get bogged down on this theory. Discuss briefly what it means and note that it is only a possible explanation of the origins of the universe, not a scientifically verifiable fact, despite what some textbooks say. Do not attempt to show the weaknesses of the theory unless you are well versed on the subject, but you can encourage students who wish to pursue the subject further to consult some of the books listed below.

While we call the arguments for the existence of God "proofs," they are not overwhelming and irresistible, probably because God expects a certain amount of faith from us. We cannot prove everything about our Faith. There are some things—the Trinity, for example—that remain a mystery; we accept these things on faith and we cannot force others to believe them. So, too, with the arguments for the existence of God. The catechist's task is to present these "proofs" in a reasonable and convincing way and then leave it up to the Holy Spirit to give a person the faith to accept them.

The material on Adam and Eve in chapter 16 (both in the text and in the manual) should be consulted in preparation for this class since the students usually ask about the Genesis account of creation.

Topics for Discussion:

1. What are some examples of atheism in the world today?
2. Is there a conflict between science and religion?
3. Which proof would you choose to show the existence of God to a non-believer?
4. Give some examples of design and order in the universe.

Some Questions and Answers:

1. Can a person truly be an atheist?
A. It seems unlikely. Those who most vociferously pro-

claim their atheism cast doubt on their own credibility. For why would anyone be so adamant in arguing against something they insist does not even exist? Why wouldn't a person who says there is no God be content to let others believe what they want? Perhaps those who call themselves atheists rant and rave against belief in God because, deep down, they realize how far out of step they are with the evidence of their own senses. Of far greater concern than this tiny minority of intellectual atheists are the millions of practical atheists—those who say that they believe in God but who live as if God did not exist.

2. Some scientists contend that the universe is the product of pure chance. How would you answer them?

A. To say that the universe happened by chance makes as much sense as saying that the presidential figures on Mount Rushmore were carved out by the wind and rain. Or that a computer resulted when thousands of pieces of wood and metal, plastic and rubber were thrown haphazardly into the air and came down perfectly assembled. If the universe were the result of blind chance, how is it that the astronauts can plan their space flights with such precision and accuracy? Or that astronomers can predict to the minute an eclipse due a century from now? It makes much more sense to accept a universe with an intention and with someone to guide its development, but these scientists have already made up their minds, and they refuse to acknowledge any facts that would contradict their faulty premise.

3. Is evolution a demonstrable scientific fact?

A. No, evolution is a possible theory that attempts to show that human beings evolved from lower forms of life. But no one has ever found the "missing link"—that combination of animal and human that would establish a definite link between the two species. And, as indicated in some of the books listed below, there is a growing body of material that casts further doubt on the evolutionary hypothesis. But even if the evolution of the world from pre-existing and living matter should ever be proved, there would still be the need for a prime mover or first cause who started the world in motion and planned its development that way. While Catholics could accept an evolutionary theory that had God at the beginning, they could never accept the concept of atheistic evolution, which denies the existence of a first cause and says that everything evolved by chance from nothing.

Projects:

1. Trace your family tree back as far as you can.

2. Read one of the five books on evolution mentioned below and list three problems with the theory.

3. Read the Genesis account of creation and write a newspaper story describing the temptation of Adam and Eve by Satan as if you were a reporter assigned to cover the story.

References:

Catechism of the Catholic Church
Behe, Michael J. *Darwin's Black Box*
Denton, Michael. *Evolution: A Theory in Crisis*
Drummey, James J. *Catholic Replies*
Hardon, John A., S.J. *The Catholic Catechism*
_____. *Modern Catholic Dictionary*
_____. *The Question and Answer Catholic Catechism*
John Paul II, Pope. *Fides et Ratio*
Johnson, Philip E. *Darwin on Trial*
_____. *Defeating Darwinism by Opening Minds*
Johnston, George Sim. *Did Darwin Get It Right?*
Kreeft, Peter. *Fundamentals of the Faith*
_____. and Tacelli, Ronald K. *Handbook of Christian Apologetics*
Most, William. *Catholic Apologetics Today*
Nevins, Albert J., M.M., *Catholicism: The Faith of Our Fathers*
Pius XII, Pope. *Humani Generis*
Sheed, Frank. *Theology for Beginners*
Stoddard, John. *Rebuilding a Lost Faith*
Stravinskas, Rev. Peter M.J. *The Catholic Answer Book*
_____. *The Catholic Answer Book 2*

Chapter 3

The Place of Religion in Our Life

Purpose: The purpose of this chapter is to show that religion is natural and necessary for us and that one religion is not as good or true as another.

Tips for Teachers: Begin the class by establishing a definition for religion. You can illustrate it by writing the word "God" high on the board and the word "us" low on the board. Then draw a line between the two words to show our relationship of dependence on God. Next, get into the question of religion being natural and necessary to people throughout history, noting that millions of people, including Christians and Jews, believe that God has revealed what he expects of us. Define the term "revelation" and all the terms used so there will be no confusion about the meaning or understanding of words.

The most fundamental point to be discussed, however, is whether one religion is as good as another. You may find some students who will say that it does not make any difference what a person's religious affiliation is. Put on the board the sentence "One _____ is as good as another." Fill in the blank with various words, such as car, sports team, song, or prom date, and ask how many agree with each sentence. There will be considerable disagreement.

Then insert the word "religion" and ask why this word should be any different from the others. If it makes a difference whom one chooses to take to the prom, it certainly ought to make a difference what religion one chooses to follow, especially since there are many contradictions among religions. Ask the students how two religions with completely opposite beliefs can be equally true and reliable.

Make sure you emphasize that you are talking about the objective teachings of certain religions and not the subjective consciences of their followers. Point out that while one may disagree with a person's religious views, one should always show charity toward the person. But also cite the statements of Vatican II and Pope John XXIII about the necessity of always affirming the truth and opposing religious indifference.

This is a delicate chapter, so handle it carefully. Some people find it almost impossible to see the distinction between the error and the person in error, so you may have to go over the same ground more than once. It would also be helpful to read chapter 14 before giving this class for additional insight into the relationship of the Catholic Church to other churches.

You can sum up the whole class by noting that there are hundreds of different religions today and that you will start the search for the truest and most reliable one with Christianity because of its numbers and its influence on human history.

Topics for Discussion:

1. Why is religion necessary for us?
2. Is one religion as good or true as another?
3. Opinion polls show that less than 40 percent of American adults interviewed had attended church the previous seven days. Why do you think the percentage is so low?
4. If a primitive tribe had never heard of the Ten Commandments, would its members still observe similar moral principles?

Some Questions and Answers:

1. What is wrong with religious indifference, with believing that it does not matter what religion a person follows?

A. Religious indifference implies that there is no such thing as objective truth, that truth and falsehood are equally pleasing to God, and that God, who has revealed to us certain truths to help us get to heaven, does not really care whether we accept those truths or not.

2. Can we assume that those whom we believe to be in objective error about religious matters will not go to heaven?

A. No, we cannot assume any such thing. We must distinguish between the error and the person in error. We should make every attempt, using charity and good will, to show such a person the truth and leave it up to God to decide whether that person is sincere and conscientious in seeking the truth and whether he or she will get to heaven.

3. Catholics are frequently accused of imposing their religious and moral views on others by speaking out on such issues as abortion, divorce, and homosexuality. How would you answer this accusation?
A. As citizens of a country, Catholics have as much right as anyone else to express their views on important moral issues. The true meaning of a pluralistic society is one in which all points of view are aired and debated with the hope that decisions will be made in accord with the will of God, the ultimate Author of all laws and the Ruler of all governments. As people of God, Catholics have a solemn obligation to work for a society that is oriented toward God.

Projects:

1. Look up in a current almanac the religious population of the United States and of the world. List the five major religious denominations in the order of their size.

2. Look up in a current Catholic almanac the section on the Protestant and Orthodox churches. Summarize the beliefs of one denomination.

3. Read articles 8 and 14-16 in Vatican II's *Dogmatic Constitution on the Church* and list the most important points covered.

References:

Catechism of the Catholic Church
Currie, David. *Born Fundamentalist, Born-Again Catholic*
Catholic Almanac
Drummey, James J. *Catholic Replies*
Duggan, G. H. *Beyond Reasonable Doubt*
Flannery, Austin. *Vatican Council II: The Conciliar and Post-Conciliar Documents* (2 vols.)

Fox, Rev. Robert J. *Protestant Fundamentalism and the Born-Again Catholic*
Hahn, Scott and Kimberly. *Rome Sweet Home*
Index of Watchtower Errors. Edited by David A. Reed
Keating, Karl. *Catholicism and Fundamentalism*
Most, William. *Catholic Apologetics Today*
Nevins, Albert J., M.M. *Answering a Fundamentalist*
_____. *Catholicism: The Faith of Our Fathers*
_____. *Strangers at Your Door*
Surprised by Truth. Edited by Patrick Madrid
Whalen, William. *Faiths for the Few*
_____. *Separated Brethren*
_____. *Strange Gods*

Chapter 4

The Gospels in Our Life

Purpose: The purpose of this chapter is to show that the New Testament in general, and the Gospels in particular, are reliable sources of information about the origins of Christianity.

Tips for Teachers: Begin the class by listing on the board the seven questions at the beginning of the chapter. Then go through them one by one, trying to draw as much information as possible from the students. Put special emphasis on the historical and archaeological evidence that has confirmed the authenticity of the Gospels. H. V. Morton's book, *In the Steps of the Master*, will be very helpful. The catechist should also watch for new archaeological findings, such as the skeleton of the crucified man that was discovered in 1968 and the tomb of the high priest Caiaphas that was uncovered in 1990 on the western outskirts of Jerusalem.

Topics for Discussion:

1. Can we get reliable historical facts from the Gospels?
2. Why have scholars studied the New Testament more than any other written work?
3. What is the most convincing evidence that the Gospels are authentic history?

Some Questions and Answers:

1. Have any contradictions ever been found between the Gospels and other historical sources covering the same period?
A. No. Whenever events narrated in the Gospels have been compared with other histories of the time, the Gospels are always in accord with those histories. Not a single contradiction has ever been found.

2. What are some of the sciences that have been involved in verifying the accuracy of the Gospels?

A. Research into the accuracy of the Gospels has been undertaken by scholars in such fields as archaeology, astronomy, chemistry, geology, meteorology, physics, and seismology.

3. Don't some Scripture scholars contend that the Gospels may have been written by persons other than Matthew, Mark, Luke, and John?

A. Yes, some do make this contention on the grounds that the internal evidence—the vocabulary, style, and theological expressions contained in the Gospels—suggests different authors. But this is a very subjective way of looking at the authorship of the Gospels, and it goes against the objective historical evidence. For instance, there is the second-century work of St. Irenaeus, who in his youth was a pupil of St. Polycarp, who had known John the Apostle. Writing in *Against Heresies*, Irenaeus said:

> Matthew also issued among the Hebrews a written Gospel in their own language, while Peter and Paul were evangelizing in Rome and laying the foundation of the Church. After their departure, Mark, the disciple and interpreter of Peter, also handed down to us in writing what had been preached by Peter. Luke also, the companion of Paul, set down in a book the Gospel preached by him. Afterwards, John, the disciple of the Lord who reclined at his bosom, also published a Gospel while he was residing at Ephesus in Asia.

4. What are the Dead Sea Scrolls?

A. The Dead Sea Scrolls are a collection of manuscripts, written mostly in Hebrew, that were discovered in caves near the Dead Sea beginning in 1947. Dating from the first century before and the first century after Christ, the scrolls contain fragments of virtually every book of the Old Testament, including a complete text of Isaiah, as well as writings about the Essenes, a strict Jewish sect that lived in that region from the second century B.C. to the second century A.D. The scrolls, which are also known as the Qumran Manuscripts, have been intensively studied by Bible scholars since their discovery.

Projects:

1. Look up some information on the Dead Sea Scrolls in an encyclopedia or in the *Reader's Guide to Periodical Literature* at the library.

2. Do a report on the life of one of the four evangelists.

References:

Catechism of the Catholic Church
Catholic Almanac
Daniel-Rops, Henri. *Daily Life in the Time of Jesus*
Dictionary of Saints. Edited by John J. Delaney
Drummey, James J. *Catholic Replies*
Duggan, G. H. *Beyond Reasonable Doubt*
Encyclopedia of Catholic History. Edited by Matthew
      Bunson
Fuentes, Antonio. *A Guide to the Bible*
Graham, Henry G. Where We Got the Bible
Jurgens, William. *The Faith of the Early Fathers* (3 vols.)
Keller, Werner. *The Bible as History*
McKenzie, John L. *Dictionary of the Bible*
Morton, H. V. *In the Steps of the Master*
Most, William. *Catholic Apologetics Today*
_____. *Free From All Error*
Nevins, Albert J., M.M. *Catholicism: The Faith of Our
      Fathers*
Pontifical Biblical Commission. *The Historicity of the Gos-
      pels*
Ricciotti, Guiseppe. *The Life of Christ* (Chapters 1-13)
Ruffin, Bernard. *The Twelve: The Lives of the Apostles
      After Calvary*
Stravinskas, Rev. Peter M.J. *The Catholic Church and the
      Bible*
Vatican II, *Dogmatic Constitution on Divine Revelation*

Chapter 5

The Man Who Cannot Be Ignored

Purpose: The purpose of this chapter is to show that Jesus Christ claimed to be God and that he was a stable, competent, and trustworthy Person.

Tips for Teachers: This chapter provides a marvelous opportunity to paint a stirring and unforgettable portrait of Jesus by discussing the many virtues and admirable qualities that have drawn hundreds of millions of people to him over the past 2,000 years. So many examples of Jesus' flawless personality can be taken from the Gospels that catechists whose schedule permits would be well-advised to spend two or three or even more classes on this chapter.

The Person of Jesus is "at the heart of catechesis," Pope John Paul said in *On Catechesis in Our Time*, because "the whole of Christ's life was a continual teaching: his silences, his miracles, his gestures, his prayer, his love for people, his special affection for the little and the poor, his acceptance of the total sacrifice on the cross for the redemption of the world, and his resurrection are the actualization of his word and the fulfillment of revelation" (nn. 5, 9).

The class may be opened by asking the students for examples of Jesus' influence in the modern world. For example, no other person has his birthday celebrated throughout the world; no one sends Washington's Birthday cards or gives Abraham Lincoln presents; no one sings carols about Mount Vernon as we sing or hear them sung about Bethlehem. Numerous other examples can be found to demonstrate that Jesus is an important historical figure. Teachers may summarize this importance by having a student read "One Solitary Life" on pages 39-40 of the text.

The next step involves showing that Jesus claimed to be God. Use some of the examples in the book and have the students present them in story form. A life of Christ will give you the background for these incidents in Jesus' life. You may put the chart on page 42 on the board as a way of illustrating that Jesus could not have been just a good man. Some of the topics suggested below will help promote this discussion.

The remainder of the class or classes should draw heavily on the Gospels for examples of Jesus' mental competence, his debating skill, his storytelling mastery, his moral code, and his qualities of mercy, compassion, love, forgiveness, courage, and fearlessness. Assign the students Scripture passages and ask them to find examples of these attributes of Christ. The possibilities for developing this chapter are many, and catechists should take good advantage of them.

One method of stimulating discussion about Jesus is to give the class a series of true/false questions and then use those questions to cover the principal points in the chapter. For instance:

_____ Jesus has not had much influence on history (F).
_____ Jesus was as much a human being as we are (T).
_____ Jesus never said he was God (F).
_____ Jesus freely decided to die on the cross (T).
_____ Jesus never sinned, but he was tempted (T).
_____ Jesus was not a good debater or storyteller (F).
_____ Jesus' moral teachings are too hard to follow (F).
_____ Jesus has made a difference in my life (?).

Topics for Discussion:

1. Give some examples of Jesus' influence in the world today.

2. Did Jesus ever claim to be God, to be a divine messenger?

3. Is it possible that Jesus was only a good man?

4. Give some examples of his mental capability, moral code, storytelling prowess, or his personal qualities.

5. What difference would it make if Jesus never came to earth?

6. If you knew that Jesus was coming to earth again next month, and you were given the opportunity to advise him beforehand, where would you tell him to appear and in what occupation or station in life? Do you think he would be any

more successful in recruiting followers this time than he was the first time?

Some Questions and Answers:

1. What do the initials A.D. mean?

A. In Latin, A.D. means *anno Domini*, in the year of our Lord. Thus, the year in which we live is dated from the year in which Jesus was born. The time before Christ was born is called B.C.

2. Did the evangelists tell us everything they knew about Jesus?

A. No. They told us as much as we needed to know to follow Jesus, but John, at the end of his Gospel, said that "there are still many other things that Jesus did, yet if they were written about in detail, I doubt there would be room enough in the entire world to hold the books to record them" (21:25). John did not mean this literally, of course, but it is an indication that many things were left out. For example, we know nothing about the first thirty years of Jesus' life except for his birth and the time he was lost in the temple at age twelve.

3. What is a parable and why did Jesus preach that way?

A. A parable is a story told to illustrate a supernatural truth. Jesus taught this way because the people of the time could understand difficult truths better than if he simply lectured to them. He used examples of people, places, and events that were familiar to his listeners. The theme running through most of his parables was the kingdom of God. Whether Christ was talking about laborers in the vineyard, the mustard seed, the good shepherd, the sower and the seed, the wise and foolish virgins, or the vine and the branches, he was pointing out what the kingdom would be like, what it would take to reach it, and that many would be lost on the way.

4. Some people claim that Jesus only gradually came to understand that he was the Messiah. Is this true?

A. No, it is not true, and this notion was condemned as false by Pope St. Pius X in 1907. Agreeing with his predecessor at a general audience in 1990, Pope John Paul declared that Jesus first proclaimed his Messiahship publicly in the temple at the age of twelve when he told Mary and Joseph, "Did you not know that I had to be in my Father's house?" (Luke 2:49).

This response, said John Paul, was our Lord's "manifestation of his awareness that he was 'the Son of God' and thus of his duty to be 'in his Father's house,' the temple, to 'take care of his Father's business' (according to another translation of the Gospel phrase). Thus, Jesus publicly declared, perhaps for the first time, his Messiahship and his divine identity." (Cf. *Catechism of the Catholic Church*, nn. 472-474)

Projects:

1. Write a short story putting the Good Samaritan in a modern-day situation.

2. Stage a play based on the Prodigal Son, the Good Samaritan, the woman caught in adultery, or another parable or incident in the life of Jesus.

3. List ten things Jesus told us to do or not do in the Sermon on the Mount (cf. Matthew 5-7).

4. Explain the meaning of two of the eight Beatitudes.

5. Write a short article about something Jesus did as if you were a newspaper reporter on the scene. For example:

GALILEAN DRIVES MERCHANTS OUT OF TEMPLE

Jerusalem, April 5 – A man from Galilee stormed into the temple today, overturned tables used by the moneychangers, and chased them out of the courtyard with a whip. According to eyewitnesses, the man is reported to have shouted at the moneychangers, "Scripture has it, 'My house shall be called a house of prayer,' but you are turning it into a den of thieves."

Little is known about the man, who goes by the name Jesus, or about the motives for his actions. The practice of selling oxen, sheep, and doves in the temple precincts, and changing coins, has become commonplace in recent years and, while some Pharisees have expressed objections to this use of a house of worship, no attempts have been made to curb it.

The Galilean was asked by what authority he had expelled the traders from the temple. He responded cryptically, "Destroy this temple and in three days I will raise it up." One observer noted that "the temple took forty-six years to construct, so it is inconceivable that anyone could rebuild it in three days."

Despite this exaggerated talk, Jesus seems to be a man of strong convictions. Some of those at the temple today expressed the opinion that Jerusalem had not heard the last of him.

References:

Catechism of the Catholic Church
Drummey, James J. Catholic Replies
Daniel-Rops, Henri. Jesus and His Times (2 vols.)
Duggan, G. H. Beyond Reasonable Doubt
Hardon, John A., S.J. The Catholic Catechism
_____. The Question And Answer Catholic Catechism
Kreeft, Peter. Letters to Jesus (Answered)
_____. and Tacelli, Ronald K. Handbook of Christian
    Apologetics
Most, William. Catholic Apologetics Today
_____. The Consciousness of Christ
Nevins, Albert J., M.M. Catholicism: The Faith of Our
    Fathers
Oursler, Fulton. The Greatest Story Ever Told
Ricciotti, Giuseppe. The Life of Christ
Sheed, Frank. To Know Christ Jesus
_____. What Difference Does Jesus Make?
Sheen, Fulton. Life of Christ

Chapter 6

The Divinity of Christ

Purpose: The purpose of this chapter is to show that Jesus is God. This can be done by looking at the Old Testament prophecies he fulfilled, the prophecies he made himself, and the miracles he performed.

Tips for Teachers: Like the previous chapter, which provided an excellent chance to explore and understand the humanity of Jesus, this chapter offers a valuable opportunity to delve into the divinity of Christ and to discuss the always fascinating subject of miracles. Because there is a wealth of pertinent material available, more than one class could be spent on this chapter.

The first part of the class should deal with prophecies—those that Jesus fulfilled from the Old Testament and the predictions he made himself. Define the term "prophecy" and demonstrate that Jesus is the only Person ever to have had his biography written centuries before he was born. Then go into the predictions of the future which Jesus made, especially his startling prophecy that Jerusalem would be destroyed. You can show how devastatingly true this prediction was by referring to the eyewitness account of Josephus, the Jewish historian, either in his own writings or as quoted in H. V. Morton's *In the Steps of the Master*.

Having covered the intellectual miracles known as prophecies, you may now treat the physical miracles Jesus performed. The four-point definition should be put on the board and there should be some preliminary discussion of the possibility of miracles, their relation to science, and whether they occur today. It would be helpful at this point if the students had been assigned to read and report on some of the miracles related in the Gospels, e.g., the cure of the blind man (John 9:1-41), the raising of Lazarus (John 11:1-44), the changing of water into wine (John 2:1-11), and the multiplication of the loaves and fishes (John 6:1-13). Students could be assigned to write a newspaper story reporting on a miracle (see the example below).

The catechist should also discuss the reasons why Jesus performed miracles, including the intention to prove his divinity. Conclude by stating that, since we can show that Jesus is God, then we must listen to what he has to say, and that the true religion we are seeking has been narrowed down to one of the Christian religions.

Topics for Discussion:

1. What is a prophecy? Which of Christ's was the most remarkable and why?

2. A best-selling book some years ago contended that Jesus conformed his life to fit the prophecies concerning the Messiah. Is this possible?

3. What is a miracle? Can science disprove miracles?

4. Do miracles occur today? Where?

Some Questions and Answers:

1. Why did Jesus perform miracles?

A. For several reasons—to show the power of God to alleviate suffering, to invite people to believe in him, to prove his divinity, and to confirm his teachings (the multiplication of the loaves and fishes illustrated the doctrine of the Eucharist).

2. Did Jesus' enemies ever deny that he performed miracles?

A. No, they could not deny what they actually witnessed with their own eyes. Instead, they either accused Jesus of performing his wonders with the help of evil spirits, or they criticized him for doing good works on the Sabbath, in violation of the Mosaic law. Neither criticism was valid, but it showed the lengths to which the enemies of Christ were willing to go to discredit our Lord.

3. Are there people today who would refuse to believe in miracles even if they witnessed one?

A. Yes, there are those who are so convinced that miracles are impossible that it seems nothing can convince them otherwise. C. S. Lewis, the great Christian apologist, once said of such people:

"If the end of the world appeared in all the literal trappings of the apocalyptic vision of the Book of Revelation, if the modern materialist saw with his own eyes the heavens rolled up and a great white throne appearing, if he had the sensation of being himself hurled into the lake of fire, he would continue forever, in that lake itself, to regard his experience as an illusion, and to find the explanation of it in psychoanalysis or cerebral pathology."

4. If Jesus was sinless, why was he baptized by John?

A. Jesus was indeed sinless and had no need of baptism, but perhaps he wanted to confirm that John the Baptist's ministry was authentic and to provide an example for the people. Recall that John at first tried to refuse Jesus' request, saying that "I should be baptized by you." But our Lord answered, "Give in for now. We must do this if we would fulfill all of God's demands" (Matthew 3:14-15). Our Lord was also foreshadowing the spiritual power of water to wash away original sin in the sacrament of Baptism.

5. Was it ever possible for Jesus to commit a sin?

A. No, it was never possible for Jesus to commit a sin because it would have meant that God was capable of sinning against himself. Since Christ was a divine Person, whose every act was an act of God, he could not sin. "In him there is nothing sinful," said John the Evangelist (1 John 3:5). And Paul said, "For we do not have a high priest who is unable to sympathize with our weakness, but one who was tempted in every way that we are, yet never sinned" (Hebrews 4:15).

When we are tempted, our will waivers and we find ourselves leaning toward evil. There was no wavering will in Christ, no inclination toward sin, and no struggle in choosing between good and evil. Jesus had both a human will and a divine will, but as the Third Council of Constantinople (680-681) taught, his human will followed his divine will "without resistance or reluctance" (cf. *Catechism of the Catholic Church*, n. 475).

Why did Christ subject himself to temptations (Matthew 4:1-11 and Luke 22:39-46)? Perhaps to show us how to overcome them in our own lives. "Since he was himself tested through what he suffered," said Paul, "he is able to help those who are tempted" (Hebrews 2:18).

Projects:

1. Act out one of Jesus' miracles, with students playing each of the parts.

2. Write a short article about one of Jesus' miracles as if you were a reporter on the scene. For example:

BETHANY MAN RAISED FROM THE DEAD

Bethany, June 2 – In this village two miles from Jerusalem, a prominent citizen by the name of Lazarus startled friends and neighbors today by walking out of the tomb in which he had been buried four days ago after succumbing to an illness. He emerged from the tomb, according to eyewitnesses, at the bidding of Jesus of Nazareth, a close friend of Lazarus and his sisters, Martha and Mary.

This was not the first time that Jesus has been associated with unexplainable events. He has acquired a reputation for wondrous works both in Judea and in Galilee, where he worked as a carpenter before becoming a wandering preacher. The temptation to dismiss the raising of Lazarus as a wild and unsupported tale is strong, but the testimony of those who were present, including many reputable citizens of Jerusalem, could not be shaken by this reporter's skepticism.

The eyewitnesses are in agreement that Jesus and a dozen of his followers arrived in Bethany earlier today and were greeted by Mary, a sister of Lazarus, who told the Galilean, "If you had been here, my brother would never have died." Jesus, seeing Mary and many other mourners weeping, asked where Lazarus was buried and then began to cry himself.

After being taken to the tomb, he ordered the stone in

front of it removed. Martha, the other sister of Lazarus, objected, saying, "Lord, it has been four days now; surely there will be a stench." But Jesus was adamant. After the stone had been rolled away, he looked up to the heavens and was heard to say, "Father, I thank you for having heard me. I know that you always hear me, but I have said this for the sake of the crowd, that they may believe that you sent me."

Those who were present said that Jesus then called loudly, "Lazarus, come out!" And before the eyes of the incredulous crowd, the man who had apparently been dead for four days walked out of the grave, bound hand and foot with linen strips, his face wrapped in a cloth. "Untie him," Jesus said, "and let him go free."

Lazarus was then stripped of the burial cloths, the eyewitnesses said, and walked off to his home under his own power. Attempts by this reporter to reach him later were unsuccessful.

References:

Catechism of the Catholic Church
Daniel-Rops, Henri. Jesus and His Times (2 vols.)
Drummey, James J. Catholic Replies
Duggan, G. H. Beyond Reasonable Doubt
Kreeft, Peter. Fundamentals of the Faith
_____. and Tacelli, Ronald K. Handbook of Christian
     Apologetics
Morton, H. V. In the Steps of the Master
Most, William. Catholic Apologetics Today
Nevins, Albert J., M.M. Catholicism: The Faith of Our
     Fathers
Oursler, Fulton. The Greatest Story Ever Told
Ricciotti, Giuseppe. The Life of Christ
Sheed, Frank. To Know Christ Jesus
_____. What Difference Does Jesus Make?
Sheen, Fulton. Life of Christ

Chapter 7

The Passion of Christ

Purpose: The purpose of this chapter is to provide a detailed historical and medical analysis of the Passion and death of Jesus—from the agony in the garden to the placing of his body in the tomb.

Tips for Teachers: Unlike the other chapters in the book, this one can be presented in story form, with the catechist guiding the students through the almost hour-by-hour narrative of the Passion of our Lord and asking them for the names of some of the persons who played a role in the death of Christ (Judas, Barabbas, Pontius Pilate, etc.). The story can have a profound and lasting impact on the students if it is handled properly, and especially if the teacher or members of the class can make some of the visual aids suggested under projects and act out some of the scenes from Holy Thursday and Good Friday. Any pictures of the Shroud of Turin, or any slides from the Passion Play that is staged every ten years in the Bavarian town of Oberammergau, will add to the students' understanding of how much Jesus must love us to have suffered and died for our sins in such a brutal manner.

Topics for Discussion:

1. Why did Jesus choose such a brutal way to die as crucifixion?

2. Why didn't Jesus come down from the cross as his tormentors demanded? Would they have been convinced that he was God if he had come down?

3. Can you think of any modern Pontius Pilates—people who do not have the courage to do the right thing because of pressure from others? Have you ever failed to do the right thing because you feared that your friends would make fun of you?

4. What difference does Jesus' dying on the cross make in your life?

Some Questions and Answers:

1. What were the causes of Jesus' agony in the Garden of Gethsemani?

A. Physical exhaustion and violent mental disturbance, the latter caused primarily by the fact that Jesus had to take upon his sinless shoulders all the sins ever committed. Our Lord also agonized because he knew that his suffering and death would be in vain for many people.

2. What was the greatest sin of Judas —his betrayal of Jesus or the taking of his own life?

A. Neither, although both were seriously sinful actions. Judas' greatest sin was despair—the abandonment of all hope that Jesus would forgive him for what he had done.

3. Why was crucifixion such a horrible way to die?

A. Because of the violence it wreaked on the human body—the partially severed nerves in the wrists, the agonizing cramps over the entire body, and the desperate struggle to breathe as the slumping body brought on asphyxiation. Pierre Barbet's book, *A Doctor at Calvary*, offers a graphic medical explanation of this terrible form of death.

4. Why didn't the soldiers break Jesus' legs?

A. Because he was already dead and there was no need to prevent him from prolonging his life by using his legs to raise his body back up the cross so he could breathe. The stab wound that pierced our Lord's heart, causing blood and water to come out of his side, is clear evidence that Jesus was dead when he was taken down from the cross.

5. What did the letters "I.N.R.I." on the cross mean?

A. They are the Latin letters for *Iesus Nazarenus Rex Iudaeorum,* meaning, "Jesus of Nazareth, King of the Jews." Pilate ordered the inscription put on the cross in Latin, Greek, and Hebrew.

Projects:

1. Make a crown of thorns using a coat hanger shaped like a crown. Find the longest thorns you can—three inches to four inches if possible—and attach them first to the coat hanger and then to each other until you have a cap of thorns.

2. Make a scourge by using a piece of a broomhandle about eighteen inches long. Tape or attach three leather or rawhide boot laces (about eighteen inches long) to the broomhandle. At the end of each lace, tie a piece of metal such as a half-inch nut. A picture of a scourge can be found in the Echo edition of John Walsh's book, *The Shroud*.

3. Simulate the crosspiece that Jesus carried by using a six- or eight-foot length of 4" x 6" wood. Organize a procession on Good Friday, with someone carrying the crosspiece, either on your parish or school grounds, or through the streets of your city or town if permission can be obtained from city or town officials.

4. Act out one or more of the scenes from Holy Thursday and Good Friday —the Last Supper, the arrest in the Garden of Gethsemani, the trial before Caiaphas or Pilate, or the crucifixion.

References:

Barbet, Pierre. *A Doctor at Calvary*
Bishop, Jim. *The Day Christ Died*
Catechism of the Catholic Church
Daniel-Rops, Henri. *Jesus and His Times* (2 vols.)
Drummey, James J. *Catholic Replies*
Gorman, Ralph. *The Trial of Christ*
Lavoie, Gilbert R. *Unlocking the Secrets of the Shroud*
Mead, Jude. *The Hours of the Passion*
Ricciotti, Giuseppe. *The Life of Christ*
Sheed, Frank. *To Know Christ Jesus*
Sheen, Fulton. *Life of Christ*
Walsh, John. *The Shroud*
Wilson, Ian. *The Blood and the Shroud*

Chapter 8

The Greatest Miracle of All

Purpose: The purpose of this chapter is to review the historical evidence that Jesus actually rose from the dead as he predicted on many occasions.

Tips for Teachers: The catechist should begin this class by stating that the whole of Christianity rests on the resurrection. If Christ did not rise from the dead, as St. Paul said, then our religion is meaningless. The resurrection is one of the most important events in all human history, and we should be familiar with the historical and logical arguments for its authenticity.

The second step is to note the several times that Jesus predicted that he would rise from the dead. Point out the irony that while his disciples apparently did not recall these predictions, the enemies of Christ did, and they dispatched soldiers to guard his tomb.

The third step could be a narration of all the events that occurred on that first Easter Sunday. If the teacher had previously assigned the students to compile a summary of these events, they could then be asked to piece the narrative together. This will prepare the way for a discussion of the objections to the resurrection, as well as of the evidence that it actually happened.

Finally, the catechist should write on the board some of the possible explanations for the undisputed fact that the tomb was empty on the third day after the crucifixion. Have the students show the flaws in the explanations that deny Jesus rose from the dead and then have them discuss the arguments in favor of the resurrection.

Spend some time on the apparitions, emphasizing the point that all of the people who said that they saw Jesus could not have been suffering from a mass hallucination. Also, discuss the transformation of the Apostles, stressing that men do not cheerfully give up their lives unless they truly believe in someone or something, in this case the bodily resurrection of Jesus from the dead.

Topics for Discussion:

1. Did Jesus ever predict that he would rise from the dead?
2. What actually happened on that first Easter Sunday?
3. Why do you think Jesus appeared first to Mary Magdalene?
4. How do we know that the Apostles didn't steal Jesus' body?
5. What do you think is the strongest evidence that Jesus rose from the dead?
6. Does it make any difference whether Jesus rose from the dead or not?

Some Questions and Answers:

1. Why does Christianity rest on the foundation of the resurrection?
A. Unless Jesus overcame death and entered into his glory, we could not expect to reach heaven at the end of our earthly life. By rising from the dead, Jesus made credible his promise that "whoever believes in me, though he should die, will come to life" (John 11:26).

2. Some skeptics of the resurrection have suggested that Jesus was drugged and still alive when taken down from the cross, and that he expired sometime later after the Apostles had removed his body from the tomb. How would you answer this contention?
A. First, the Roman soldiers were convinced that Jesus was dead and did not break his legs. Second, the spear thrust, according to the eyewitness testimony of John and the best medical analysis, pierced the heart of Jesus, causing certain death. Third, the Apostles were much too frightened and demoralized to steal the body. Fourth, this theory does not explain the hundreds of people who saw Jesus over a forty-day period or the fact that no Apostle, despite torture and death, ever denied or repudiated the resurrection of Jesus.

3. Some theologians have contended that the body of the risen Christ was not the same body that had been placed in the tomb. What is the Church's position on this?

A. Pope Paul VI rejected this contention on April 5, 1972, saying that "Jesus really arose in his very own humanity. . . . Jesus arose with the same body he had taken from the Virgin Mary, but in a new condition, verified by a new and immortal animation which imparts to Christ's physical flesh the laws and the energies of the spirit. This marvel does not nullify the reality, but rather constitutes the new reality."

4. Were all the Apostles convinced that Jesus had risen from the dead after they saw his resurrected body?

A. No, some doubted the resurrection right up until the ascension: "The eleven disciples made their way to Galilee, to the mountain to which Jesus had summoned them. At the sight of him, those who had entertained doubts fell down in homage" (Matthew 28:16-17).

5. What is the meaning of Jesus' words to Thomas a week after the resurrection?

A. When Jesus told Thomas, "You became a believer because you saw me. Blest are those who have not seen and have believed" (John 20:29), our Lord was saying that those of us who have never seen him face to face but who believe in him are blessed in his eyes because of our faith.

Projects:

1. List the names of all those persons to whom Jesus appeared in the forty days between Easter and the ascension.

2. Draw a simple map of Palestine at the time of Christ, showing the provinces of Galilee, Samaria, and Judea and some of the places where Jesus lived and taught.

3. Write a newspaper story about the resurrection as if you were a reporter in Jerusalem at the time. For example:

BODY OF CRUCIFIED MAN MISSING

Jerusalem, April 10 – The body of a Galilean agitator who was crucified on Friday for revolutionary activities against Rome was reported missing Sunday morning from its grave near Golgotha. According to a spokesman for the Sanhedrin, the body of the man known as Jesus of Nazareth was taken down from the cross and laid in the tomb late Friday afternoon.

On Saturday, a contingent of soldiers was assigned to guard the tomb, but some of those soldiers told friends that the body of Jesus was stolen by his followers while the guards were sleeping. There have been no confirmed reports of guards being punished for sleeping at their post.

Meanwhile, the city is alive with rumors that Jesus rose from the dead and has been seen by several people. He is alleged to have appeared to several women early yesterday near the tomb, to two men walking along the road to Emmaus in the afternoon, and then to a dozen or so of his closest companions here in the city last night.

Efforts by this reporter to contact some of these people have been unsuccessful. A statement issued by the Sanhedrin noted that since the reports came from people who were known to be friends of the Galilean, "no credibility should be given to them."

Temple officials have launched a diligent search for the missing corpse, but it seems to have vanished without a trace.

References:

Catechism of the Catholic Church
Drummey, James J. *Catholic Replies*
Duggan, G. H. *Beyond Reasonable Doubt*
Kreeft, Peter and Tacelli, Ronald K. *Handbook of Christian Apologetics*
Lunn, Arnold. *The Third Day*
Nevins, Albert J., M.M. *Catholicism: The Faith of Our Fathers*
Ricciotti, Giuseppe. *The Life of Christ*
Sheed, Frank. *To Know Christ Jesus*
_____. *What Difference Does Jesus Make?*
Sheen, Fulton. *Life of Christ*

Chapter 9

The Church and the Rock

Purpose: The purpose of this chapter is to show that Jesus founded a Church to carry on his work in the world and that he placed the Apostle Peter at the head of this Church.

Tips for Teachers: Before class, put on the board the chart on page 95 that shows Christ established a Church. Leave the scriptural quotes out of the boxes. They can be filled in at the appropriate time during the class.

The first part of the class should involve a discussion of the logic of Jesus' leaving behind him an organization to carry on his work. The pertinent Bible passages should be cited to show that Jesus did in fact establish a Church. The major part of the class should focus on the selection of Peter to lead the Church, presenting in story form the incidents related in Matthew 16:15-20 and John 21:15-17. Also cite the incidents from the Acts of the Apostles showing the leadership role Peter played in the early Church. Finally, note that the Pope is the only person today who even claims to be the successor of Peter.

Teachers of high school or college students will have a good opportunity to discuss and refute the attitude prevalent among young people today that one can be a follower of Jesus and not attend church. Discussion topic No. 1 would a good way to get the class started since it should provoke some comments from the students.

As for those who think they can be good Christians without paying attention to the Church Jesus founded, remind them of the words of Pope Paul VI:

He who thinks he can remain a Christian by his own efforts, deserting the institutional bonds of the visible and hierarchical Church, or who imagines he can remain faithful to the mind of Christ by fashioning for himself a church conceived according to his own ideas, is on the wrong track, and deceives himself. He compromises and perhaps rup-

44

tures, and makes others rupture, real communion with the People of God, losing the pledge of its promises.

This would be the place to recall the old saying: "Outside the Church there is no salvation," but this is not the time to explain how it should be understood. God can save anyone as he likes, and we know how great is his wisdom and his mercy; but the fact remains that in the revelation of his love, he established Christ with his Church as a bridge, over which we must pass, leading from our unhappy lot to his salvation and to his bliss.

Topics for Discussion:

1. A college student was recently quoted as saying, "We are turned off by the church but turned on by Jesus." Having read this chapter, how would you respond to that statement?

2. Why would Jesus choose someone like Peter to lead the Church when Peter had shown such weakness at times?

3. Do you see any significance in the fact that Jesus asked Peter three times if he loved him?

4. What are some examples of the authority that Peter exercised in the early years of the Church?

Some Questions and Answers:

1. Do we have any evidence that Peter was the first Bishop of Rome and the first Pope?

A. Church tradition has it that Peter was martyred (crucified upside down at his own request) in Rome between A.D. 64 and 67. Recent archaeological findings of the tomb of St. Peter under the basilica named for him in Rome confirm that he died in that city. For details of the archaeological discoveries, see Margherita Guarducci's book, *The Tomb of St. Peter*, and John Walsh's book, *The Bones of St. Peter*.

2. Can anyone besides the Bishop of Rome be the Pope?

A. No. The man who physically or spiritually (in case of exile) governs the territory that Peter once governed is the chief shepherd of the Church. By the way, a man becomes Pope by reason of his election as Bishop of Rome, not the other way around.

3. How long has the Bishop of Rome been called the Pope?

A. The title of Pope, which means "father," came into use in the sixth century, but the office had existed since the time of Jesus. The Pope's full title is Bishop of Rome, Vicar of Jesus Christ, Successor of the Prince of the Apostles, Supreme Pontiff of the Universal Church, Patriarch of the West, Primate of Italy, Archbishop and Metropolitan of the Roman Province, Sovereign of the State of Vatican City, Servant of the Servants of God.

4. Have the Popes had much influence on the course of human affairs over the past 2,000 years?

A. They most certainly have. In the words of Eric John, editor of *The Popes: A Concise Biographical History*: "No one interested in the traditional inheritance shared by the whole Western world can ignore the history of the papacy. In all the great movements—the preservation of literacy after the fall of the Roman Empire, the revival of learning, the emergence of the nation state, the rise of totalitarian democracy—on all the great occasions—the Investiture Contest, the Reformation, the French Revolution, the challenge of Communism—the Pope of the day has played some part."

5. How do you answer the objection that since the Greek word for Peter is *petros*, which means a small stone, Jesus must have founded the Church on himself, not on Peter?

A. Before Matthew's Gospel was translated into Greek, it was in Aramaic, the language spoken by Jesus. The Aramaic name for Peter is Cephas, which is a transliteration of the Aramaic word *Kepha*. What Jesus said in Matthew 16:18 was, "You are *Kepha*, and on this *kepha* I will build my church."

While you can use *kepha* in both places in Aramaic, Greek nouns have masculine and feminine endings. It's all right to use *petra* for rock, but since *petra* is feminine it can't be used for a masculine name and has to be changed to *Petros*, an already-existing Greek word meaning a small stone. Actually, the common Greek word for a small stone is *lithos*, so those who translated the Bible into Greek should have rendered Matthew 16:18, "You are *Lithos*, and on this *petra* I will build my church."

But that would have distorted the point Matthew was trying to make, namely that Peter was the rock or foundation of the church Jesus was establishing. The French have it correctly, using the word *pierre* both for Peter's name and for the rock. And the New American Bible also tries to keep the sense of what Jesus was saying by translating Matthew 16:18 as "You are 'Rock,' and on this rock I will build my church."

Projects:

1. Look up in an almanac a list of all those who have held the office of Pope. Name the first five and the last five.
2. Write a paper on the life of one Pope.
3. Start a prayer club for the Holy Father.

References:

Carroll, Warren. *The Founding of Christendom*
Catechism of the Catholic Church
Drummey, James J. *Catholic Replies*
Duggan, G. H. *Beyond Reasonable Doubt*
Encyclopedia of Catholic History. Edited by Matthew
         Bunson
Guarducci, Margherita. *The Tomb of St. Peter*
Hughes, Philip. *A Popular History of the Catholic Church*
Jaki, Stanley. *The Keys of the Kingdom*
John Paul II, Pope. *Crossing the Threshold of Hope*
Keating, Karl. *Catholicism and Fundamentalism*
Kreeft, Peter and Tacelli, Ronald K. *Handbook of Christian
         Apologetics*
Most, William. *Catholic Apologetics Today*
Nevins, Albert J., M.M. *Catholicism: The Faith of Our
         Fathers*
Oursler, Fulton and Armstrong, April. *The Greatest Faith
         Ever Known*
Walsh, John. *The Bones of St. Peter*

Chapter 10

Where Is Christ's Church Today?

Purpose: The purpose of this chapter is to show that the Church of Christ must be one and holy, and that only the Catholic Church fulfills these conditions completely.

Tips for Teachers: There is a great deal of material in this chapter, enough for more than one class, so the teacher should plan accordingly. The class could begin with a general discussion of how the Church of Christ can be recognized today, with the chart of the four marks on page 100 being put on the board. The marks should be taken up individually, spending as much time as necessary on each one.

Students should be reminded throughout this discussion that charity towards those of other religions is essential. This means, as we noted in chapter 3, always distinguishing between error and the person in error. Catechists should refer frequently to the documents of Vatican II, as well as to recent papal statements, so that students may clearly understand the position of the Catholic Church.

Regarding the mark of unity, teachers should discuss this quality as it applies to doctrine, worship, and government, bringing in the words of Christ and using the chart on page 103. The mark of holiness can be developed in different ways, emphasizing saints or miracles or the holy lives led by many Catholics today, or all three. The catechist should acquaint the students with the lives of some of the great saints in the Church, relying on some of the sources listed under references. Or students could be encouraged to write a paper on their patron saint.

Students are usually fascinated by a discussion of modern-day miracles, examples of which are plentiful. After noting that Christ said that miracles would be a sign of his Church, go over the definition of a miracle again as it was spelled out in chapter 6 and relate it to the miracles occurring today at such places as Lourdes and other shrines to the Blessed Mother. Outline the elaborate and complicated process involved in authenticating a cure at Lourdes and then having it certified as a miracle. Ruth Cranston's book, *The Miracle of Lourdes*, will be very helpful here.

Finally, take up the question of Catholics who appear to be anything but holy, stressing that the Church should be judged by those who follow all of its teachings, not by those who fail to do so.

Topics for Discussion:

1. We know that Jesus founded a Church, but how do we find that Church today?

2. How do we know that the Church of Christ must have unity, and what do we mean by unity of government, worship, and belief?

3. Does the criticism of the Pope and the Church by some Catholics mean that the Catholic Church has lost its characteristic of unity?

4. What do we mean when we say that the Church of Christ must be holy in its members?

5. Can you think of some Catholics whose holiness is an example to other people?

6. Do the cures reported at various places in the world today meet the four conditions for a miracle?

7. If you were arrested as a Catholic, would there be enough evidence to convict you?

Some Questions and Answers:

1. Were saints ivory-tower people who were out of touch with the real world?

A. Far from it. The saints whose lives we study and try to imitate were real people—flesh and blood men and women, boys and girls who experienced victory and defeat, joy and sadness, sickness and death. Like the rest of us, they were subject to temptations, but they persevered and overcame them. They were sinners who kept on trying. Saints have come from all walks of life. They have been religious and laity, intellectuals and illiterates, rich and poor. One was a barber, another a juggler, another a dressmaker. Their common bond was their great love for God and others.

2. Does the fact that there are sinners in the Church mean that the Church is sinful?

A. There are sinners in the Church, but to describe as sinful what St. Paul called "the body of Christ" (1 Corinthians 12:27) would be wrong. The Catholic Church, said Vatican II, "is holy in a way which can never fail. For Christ, the Son of God, who with the Father and the Spirit is praised as being 'alone holy,' loved the Church as his Bride, delivering himself up for her. This he did that he might sanctify her. He united her to himself as his own body and crowned her with the gift of the Holy Spirit, for God's glory" (*Constitution on the Church,* n. 39).

Pope Paul VI, in his Credo of the People of God, also talked about the holiness of the Church, saying that the Holy Spirit "gives her life and movement. She is therefore holy, though she has sinners in her bosom, because she herself has no other life but that of grace: it is by living by her life that her members are sanctified; it is by removing themselves from her life that they fall into sins and disorders that prevent the radiation of her sanctity."

Projects:

1. Write a paper on the life of your patron saint.
2. Do a book report on one of the references listed below.
3. Research the work of Catholic missionaries in foreign lands and write a paper describing the daily activities of a missionary.
4. Write a prayer for the missions and say it every day.

References:

Carroll, Warren. *The Building of Christendom*
Catechism of the Catholic Church
Ciszek, Walter, S.J. *He Leadeth Me*
Clifford, John. *In the Presence of My Enemies*
Cranston, Ruth. *The Miracle of Lourdes*
Cruz, Joan. *Eucharistic Miracles*

_____. *Relics*
Dictionary of Saints. Edited by John J. Delaney
de Wohl, Louis. *Lay Siege to Heaven* (St. Catherine of Siena)
Drummey, James J. *Catholic Replies*
Encyclopedia of Catholic History. Edited by Matthew
      Bunson
Freze, Michael, S.F.O. *The Making of Saints*
Frossard, Andre. *Forget Not Love: The Passion of Maximil-
      ian Kolbe*
Fulda, Edeltraud. *And I Shall Be Healed*
Kerrison, Raymond. *Bishop Walsh of Maryknoll*
Kreeft, Peter. *Fundamentals of the Faith*
_____. and Tacelli, Ronald K. *Handbook of Christian
      Apologetics*
McInerny, Ralph. *Miracles*
Most, William. *Catholic Apologetics Today*
Nevins, Albert J., M.M. *Catholicism: The Faith of Our
      Fathers*
Werfel, Franz. *The Song of Bernadette*
Wuerl, Donald. *The Forty Martyrs*

Chapter 11

Christ's Church—
Catholic and Apostolic

Purpose: The purpose of this chapter is to show that the Church of Christ must be catholic (universal) and apostolic, and that only the Catholic Church fulfills these conditions completely.

Tips for Teachers: Continuing the discussion of ways to recognize the Church of Christ today, the catechist should take up the mark of catholicity, using the chart on page 116 and talking about the worldwide travels of recent Popes. Coverage of this mark should include mention of the persecutions, invasions, revolutions, and major heresies which the Church has survived only because Jesus has been with her, as he promised, from the beginning. Some helpful materials are listed under references.

The other part of this chapter deals with the apostolic nature of the Catholic Church, both in being able to trace its leaders back to the Apostles and in teaching today exactly the same doctrines taught by the Apostles. A comparison of the Apostles' Creed and the Nicene Creed with Pope Paul's *Credo of the People of God* (cf. chapter 24) demonstrates the fidelity of the leaders of today's Church with the teachings of the early Church. These Creeds, Pope John Paul II said, are "an exceptionally important expression of the living heritage placed in the custody of the pastors" of the Catholic Church (*On Catechesis in Our Time*, n. 28).

Recall again the claims of recent Popes to be the successor of St. Peter and, in a spirit of truth and charity, call attention to the many beliefs and teachings of Christ which must be held by any church that claims to be his Church. The Catholic Church is indeed the cornerstone of Christendom, and the evidence of this must be made clear to the students. This is a wonderful opportunity to show them how strong and reasonable is our conviction that the Catholic Church is the Church founded by Jesus Christ to carry on his work in the world.

Topics for Discussion:

1. What do we mean when we say that the Church of Christ must be catholic or universal?

2. How have recent Popes fulfilled the command of Jesus to "go into the whole world and proclaim the good news to all creation" (Mark 16:15)?

3. What do we mean when we say that the Church of Christ must be apostolic?

4. Can a religion that came into existence many centuries after Christ be the religion he started?

Some Questions and Answers:

1. When was the word "Catholic" first applied to the Church of Christ?

A. The word "Catholic" was first used by St. Ignatius of Antioch around the year A.D. 107.

2. Why has the Catholic Church been described as the cornerstone of Christendom?

A. Because for ten centuries the Catholic Church was the only Christian Church. When the Protestant Reformation occurred in the sixteenth century, the Bible on which all of the reformers' beliefs were based was available to Protestants only because the Catholic Church had gathered the books of the Bible together, decided which books were authentic and which were false, and preserved the Scriptures through the centuries. Without the Catholic Church, there would be no Bible, no Christianity, and no Protestantism.

3. What are some of the teachings of Christ that must be accepted by any church claiming to be his Church?

A. Authority of the Church as well as the Bible, necessity of penance and fasting, necessity of faith and good works, the Real Presence of Jesus in the Eucharist, and the sacraments of Baptism, Confirmation, Penance, Holy Eucharist, Anointing of the Sick, Holy Orders, and Matrimony.

Projects:

1. Write a summary of a recent papal visit to the United States.
2. Look up in the almanac a list of the world's cardinals. How many countries do they represent?
3. Name ten major doctrines that are contained in the Apostles' Creed, the Nicene Creed, and the *Credo of the People of God*.

References:

Carroll, Warren. *The Building of Christendom*
_____. *The Founding of Christendom*
Catechism of the Catholic Church
Catholic Encyclopedia. Edited by Rev. Peter Stravinskas
Drummey, James J. *Catholic Replies*
Encyclopedia of Catholic History. Edited by Matthew
        Bunson
Hughes, Philip. *A Popular History of the Catholic Church*
_____. *A Popular History of the Reformation*
Jurgens, William. *The Faith of the Early Fathers* (3 vols.)
Keating, Karl. *What Catholics Believe*
Kreeft, Peter. *Fundamentals of the Faith*
_____. and Tacelli, Ronald K. *Handbook of Christian
        Apologetics*
Most, William. *Catholic Apologetics Today*
Nevins, Albert J., M.M. *Catholicism: The Faith of Our
        Fathers*
Oursler, Fulton and Armstrong, April. *The Greatest Faith
        Ever Known*

Chapter 12

The Authority of the Church

Purpose: The purpose of this chapter is to clarify the teaching of the Catholic Church on its authority and infallibility.

Tips for Teachers: Because the doctrine of infallibility is so misunderstood, catechists should take care to present it very clearly and precisely. Begin the class by using some of the discussion topics to show what infallibility *does not* mean. Then spell out the conditions for an infallible pronouncement, applying them to Pope Pius XII's pronouncement on the Assumption. Write the four conditions on the board and show how Pius XII fulfilled each of them.

The next stage involves outlining the logical reasons for the grant of this power by Christ to his Church and the scriptural evidence showing that he intended to protect his Church from ever teaching error in his name. Use the chart on page 136 to indicate again that the Catholic Church is the Church of Christ and that there is no substance to the arguments that the Catholic Church never was the Church of Christ or that it once was the true Church but fell into error. Point out, too, that it doesn't make much sense to deny infallibility to one person, the Pope, while claiming it for millions of other individuals.

Finally, stress that anyone who doubts the infallibility of the Catholic Church need only consider the indisputable historical fact that no Pope or Council has ever revoked an infallible decree of a previous Pope or Council. This absence of error over 2,000 years can only be due to the special protection of God. Cite the statement from Pope John XXIII's opening speech to the Second Vatican Council regarding the unchanging nature of the Church's teachings.

Also to be emphasized is the obligation of Catholics to give positive assent to the Church's authoritative, non-infallible teachings, such as Pope Paul VI's restatement of the

Church's opposition to artificial contraception in *Humanae Vitae*. The questions and answers below will be helpful in this area.

Topics for Discussion:

1. Does infallibility mean that the Pope cannot sin?
2. Does it mean that he cannot make a mistake when speaking on any matter—religious, political, or scientific?
3. What precisely does papal infallibility mean?
4. What New Testament passages indicate that Christ intended his Church to be infallible?
5. Can a non-Catholic logically deny infallibility to the Pope and, at the same time, claim a personal infallibility for himself in interpreting the Bible?

Some Questions and Answers:

1. What does the phrase *ex cathedra* mean?

A. It is a Latin expression meaning "from the chair" of authority. When the Pope speaks *ex cathedra* on a matter of faith or morals, he is speaking in his official capacity as the successor of St. Peter and as supreme head of the Church of Christ, which means that his pronouncement is infallible.

2. Was it an individual Pope who infallibly proclaimed himself to be infallible?

A. No, it was the First Vatican Council. On July 18, 1870, that Council approved the constitution *Pastor Aeternus*, which said that when the Pope in his official capacity makes a final decision binding the entire Church in a matter of faith and morals, the decision is infallible and immutable and does not require the prior consent of the Church.

3. Does infallibility reside only in the Pope?

A. No, it also resides in the bishops when they teach authoritatively on a matter of faith and morals while gathered in an ecumenical council or while in their respective dioceses they agree with one another and with their head, the Pope. In both cases, the bishops must act in conjunction with the Pope and with his approval.

4. What are some of the practical reasons for papal infallibility?

A. It is a necessary safeguard for the transmission of God's truths to us. Catholics must be sure that they are hearing truth and not falsehood since their eternal salvation is at stake. Christ could not remain with his Church "until the end of the world" if it could teach error or immorality in his name. If the Church of Christ were not infallible, it would imply that Christ did not care whether or not we got his message straight.

5. What is an ecumenical council?

A. An ecumenical council is an assembly of all the bishops of the world under the authority and presidency of the Pope or his representative. The Pope alone can summon an ecumenical council and he must approve its decrees before they can be promulgated. There have been twenty-one ecumenical councils from Nicea in 325 to Vatican II in the 1960s.

6. What is an encyclical and what is its binding force?

A. An encyclical is a letter written by the Pope and addressed usually to the bishops, clergy, and faithful of the Church, but sometimes to all people of good will, expressing the Holy Father's mind on a doctrinal question or on some important moral or social issue. Although encyclicals are usually not infallible pronouncements, Catholics are expected to give positive assent to them (Vatican II, *Constitution on the Church*, n. 25). Pope Pius XII, in his encyclical *Humani Generis*, put it this way:

> Nor must it be thought that what is expounded in encyclical letters does not of itself demand consent, since in writing such letters the Popes do not exercise the supreme power of their teaching authority. For these matters are taught with the ordinary teaching authority, of which it is true to say: 'He who heareth you, heareth me' (Luke 10:16); and generally what is expounded and inculcated in encyclical letters already for other reasons appertains to Catholic doctrine.
>
> But if the Supreme Pontiffs in their official documents purposely pass judgment on a matter up to that

time under dispute, it is obvious that that matter, according to the mind and will of the same Pontiffs, cannot be any longer considered a question open to discussion among theologians.

Projects:

1. Choose one ecumenical council other than Vatican II and list its principal decrees.
2. Describe briefly the subject matter of three encyclicals issued by Pope John Paul II.

References:

Burke, Cormac. *Authority and Freedom in the Church*
Catechism of the Catholic Church
Catholic Encyclopedia. Edited by Rev. Peter Stravinskas
Drummey, James J. *Catholic Replies*
Encyclopedia of Catholic History. Edited by Matthew
        Bunson
Frossard, Andre. *Portrait of John Paul II*
Hardon, John. *The Catholic Catechism*
_____. *Modern Catholic Dictionary*
_____. *The Question and Answer Catholic Catechism*
Hughes, Philip. *The Church in Crisis: A History of the
        General Councils, 325-1870*
John Paul II, Pope. *Crossing the Threshold of Hope*
_____. *Ordinatio Sacerdotalis*
Keating, Karl. *Catholicism and Fundamentalism*
Kreeft, Peter and Tacelli, Ronald K. *Handbook of Christian
        Apologetics*
Most, William. *Catholic Apologetics Today*
Nevins, Albert J., M.M. *Catholicism: The Faith of Our
        Fathers*
Pius XII, Pope. *Humani Generis*
Vatican II, *Dogmatic Constitution on the Church*
Wuerl, Donald, Lawler, Thomas and Lawler, Ronald. *The
        Catholic Catechism*
_____. *The Teaching of Christ*

Chapter 13

The Church and the Bible

Purpose: The purpose of this chapter is to show the role of the Catholic Church in preserving and promoting the Bible over the centuries, and to demonstrate the need for an infallible living interpreter of both sources of divine truth, the Bible and Tradition.

Tips for Teachers: For this class, the catechist should be familiar with Vatican II's *Constitution on Divine Revelation* and the *Catechism of the Catholic Church*, nn. 101-141. The class can be started by discussing the composition of the Bible—the books of the Old and New Testaments, when they were written, what they teach, etc. This information can be found in the Bible itself, in the *Catholic Almanac*, and in Antonio Fuentes' book *A Guide to the Bible*. Cover briefly the compilation of the Bible, noting that it was not widely available until the 15th century.

The key point of the chapter, however, is the necessity of an infallible interpreter of the Bible. Discuss the Protestant principle of private interpretation and the problems that can arise from this approach and contrast it with the Catholic position that there must be a reliable, living authority to decide disputed scriptural questions. Point out, too, that the Bible cannot be our sole religious guide since millions of people never had access to it at all, not all of its teachings are easily understood, and some Christian beliefs are not found in the Bible.

Finally, define and discuss the other source of divine revelation, Tradition, noting that it flows from the same "divine wellspring" as the Bible and also demands an authentic, living interpreter.

Topics for Discussion:

1. What is the Bible?
2. Why didn't Jesus write any lines of Scripture or instruct the Apostles to do so?

3. Give some examples to show that the Bible is an important part of Catholic life (its use in the liturgy, for example).

4. What do we mean by Tradition?

5. Why is the Bible one of the all-time best-selling books?

Some Questions and Answers:

1. Is private interpretation of the Bible reasonable?

A. No, because allowing a person to read the Bible and put whatever meaning he or she pleases on a particular passage can only lead to many different interpretations, and the numerous disagreements which have divided Christendom over the centuries. Private interpretation also implies that God had nothing specific to tell us when he inspired the human authors to write the Bible. It suggests that it did not make any difference to him how many interpretations—some even contradictory—might be forthcoming. This is why the Catholic Church insists on an infallible and living interpreter of the Holy Scriptures.

2. What do we mean when we say that the Bible is divinely inspired?

A. By divine inspiration we mean the God communicated to the human authors the ideas and teachings that he wanted to be included in the Scriptures. The choice of words and the literary style were left to the authors. In other words, God determined what should be said; the human authors decided how it should be said.

3. How do we know that the Bible is the inspired word of God?

A. We know this because the Catholic Church, which Jesus established and guaranteed would always teach the truth, tells us that the Bible is the inspired word of God. Here are the steps leading to this conclusion:

(1) If we look at the Bible as a collection of books about religious history, we find in existence today several thousand partial and complete manuscripts, in many languages, going back nearly 2,000 years. A comparison of these manuscripts with each other, with the writings of Roman and Jewish his-

torians, and with archaeological findings in the Middle East shows that the Bible gives us an accurate historical account of many persons, places, and events.

(2) If we look at the Gospels as reliable history books, they tell us about a man named Jesus who claimed to be God and proved his claim with spectacular miracles, including his own resurrection from the dead. The Gospels tell us that Jesus established a Church (Matthew 16:18), promised that it would last until the end of the world (Matthew 28:20), and said that it would always teach the truth (John 14:16-17).

(3) For about three centuries after Christ, many manuscripts were circulated as the inspired word of God. These included not only the Gospels of Matthew, Mark, Luke, and John, but also "Gospels" attributed to Peter, James, Thomas, and others. The Catholic Church ended this confusion late in the 4th century by declaring which books were truly inspired by God and which were not, giving us the same Bible that Catholics use today, with 46 books in the Old Testament and 27 in the New Testament.

(4) Not only did the Catholic Church decide the content of the Bible, but it also preserved it through the centuries and continues to be the only reliable interpreter of its passages.

4. Why can't the Bible be the sole rule of faith and the only religious guide to heaven?

A. Because Jesus never said the Bible was the only guide to heaven; because he told the Apostles to go forth and teach, not to go forth and write a book; because millions of people have lived and died without having seen or been able to read the Bible; because not everything contained in Scripture is clear and intelligible to its readers; and because the Bible does not contain all the teachings of the Christian religion. For example, such doctrines as the Immaculate Conception and the Assumption are not explicitly stated in the Bible, nor are the religious observance of Sunday or the practice of praying to the Holy Spirit.

Protestants quote St. Paul in support of this claim that the Bible is the sole rule of faith, notably his statement in 2 Timothy 3:16, where he says that "all Scripture is inspired of

God and is useful for teaching—for reproof, correction, and training in holiness." But to say that Scripture is "useful" (other translations say "profitable") is not the same thing as saying that it is the only source of truth.

5. How can Catholics rely on Tradition when Jesus and Paul both condemned tradition?

A. In Matthew 15:3 and Colossians 2:8, Jesus and Paul were referring to human traditions or customs. When Catholics use Tradition with a capital "T", they are thinking of what Paul referred to when he told the Thessalonians to "hold fast to the traditions you received from us, either by our word or by letter" (2 Thessalonians 2:15). Paul also referred to the Catholic understanding of Tradition when he told Timothy, "The things which you have heard from me through many witnesses you must hand on to trustworthy men who will be able to teach others" (2 Timothy 2:2).

6. Are Catholics required to accept every statement in the Bible as the literal truth?

A. No. For instance, Catholics are not required to believe that the earth was created in six 24-hour days. This was the human author's way of making the people of the time understand that God created the world out of nothing. Whether it took God six days or six centuries is immaterial. As St. Augustine said, the Bible tells us how to go to heaven, not how the heavens go.

It should be noted, however, that the Church encourages scholars to investigate the Scriptures carefully to see what literary forms were used, what meaning the human authors intended, and what truths God wanted to communicate through their words. The teaching authority of the Church, of course, reserves the right to determine definitively whether the interpretations of scholars and theologians are correct and whether they are worthy of belief by the faithful.

Projects:

1. Write a summary of Vatican II's *Constitution on Divine Revelation.*

2. Write a brief description of the contents of one book of the Old Testament and one book of the New Testament, using the summaries that appear in the Bible, in the *Catholic Almanac*, or in the Fuentes book.

3. Get into the habit of reading a few verses of the Bible every day.

References:

Catechism of the Catholic Church
Catholic Almanac
Drummey, James J. *Catholic Replies*
Duggan, Rev. Michael. *The Consuming Fire*
Fuentes, Antonio. *A Guide to the Bible*
Graham, Henry G. *Where We Got the Bible*
Keller, Werner. *The Bible as History*
Kreeft, Peter and Tacelli, Ronald K. *Handbook of Christian Apologetics*
McKenzie, John, L. *Dictionary of the Bible*
Most, William. *Catholic Apologetics Today*
_____. *Free From All Error*
Nevins, Albert J., M.M. *Catholicism: The Faith of Our Fathers*
Pontifical Biblical Commission. *The Historicity of the Gospels*
Stenhouse, Paul. *Catholic Answers to Bible Christians* (2 vols.)
Stravinskas, Rev. Peter M.J. *The Bible and the Mass*
_____. *The Catholic Church and the Bible*
Vatican II. *Dogmatic Constitution on Divine Revelation*

Chapter 14

The Church and Ecumenism

Purpose: The purpose of this chapter is to define and explain the concept of ecumenism, as the Catholic Church has circumscribed it, so that Catholics may participate intelligently in efforts to hasten the day when there will be one flock and one shepherd.

Tips for Teachers: Start the class by putting the word "ecumenism" on the board and then, as we did in the class on infallibility, discuss first what the term *does not* mean before establishing a precise definition. Next, get into the attitudes and characteristics that are essential to any successful ecumenical dialogue. Then, using the various statements from the documents of Vatican II, from *Principles and Norms of Ecumenism*, and from *Ut Unum Sint*, show the unique role of the Catholic Church in the plan of salvation, the relationship of the Catholic Church to other churches, and the way in which those outside the Catholic Church can also be saved. The material in the questions and answers below will be helpful.

    Note that there are still many obstacles to Christian unity but, with the help of God and our own prayer and "change of heart," it can someday be achieved. Needless to say, all of this material should be handled in a spirit of charitable truthfulness. Teachers should be on the lookout for new statements or actions by the Church in the ecumenical field so as to keep the class up to date.

    If time permits, catechists could run through the "Chain of Faith" at the end of the chapter, or it could be used at the beginning of the next class.

Topics for Discussion:

    1. Why is there such a tragic lack of unity among Christians?

    2. Give a precise definition of ecumenism.

3. Does ecumenism rule out attempts to convert people to the Catholic Church?

4. A Catholic friend, in his desire to bring about unity with other Christian religions in your area, proposes that certain basic Catholic teachings which some Protestants find hard to accept, such as papal infallibility or devotion to the Blessed Virgin, be ignored or played down. Is this a good idea?

5. Does the Catholic Church have a special place in God's plan of salvation?

6. Can a person who has never heard of God or his Church get to heaven?

Some Questions and Answers:

1. What characteristics must be present in any dialogue between Catholics and non-Catholics?

A. According to Pope Paul VI, dialogue among Christians must feature clarity and comprehension, meekness and not arrogance, trust that promotes confidence and friendship, and prudence in the manner of presentation.

2. Can anyone engage in an ecumenical dialogue?

A. No. Vatican II said that only "truly competent" persons—those thoroughly aware of the history, doctrines, and spiritual activities of the Catholic Church, as well as the history, doctrines, and spiritual activities of other Christian communities, should take part in ecumenical discussions. Good will is not enough; it must be accompanied by knowledge and understanding, too, if one hopes to overcome centuries of division and disagreement.

3. What exactly did the Second Vatican Council say about Protestant churches?

A. The Council said that the Protestant churches "became separated from full communion with the Catholic Church" centuries ago and remain in "imperfect communion" with the Catholic Church today. It also said that while these separated churches "suffer from defects" in doctrine, discipline, and structure, they do possess many "significant elements" of the Church of Christ, including the Scriptures, the life of grace, and the virtues of faith, hope, and charity. For this reason, the Council said, Protestant churches "have by no means been deprived of significance and importance in the mystery of salvation."

Nevertheless, Vatican II continued, "our separated brethren, whether considered as individuals or as Communities and Churches, are not blessed with that unity which Jesus Christ wished to bestow on all those whom he has regenerated and vivified into one body and newness of life—that unity which the holy Scriptures and the revered tradition of the Church proclaim.

"For it is through Christ's Catholic Church alone, which is the all-embracing means of salvation, that the fullness of the means of salvation can be obtained. It was to the apostolic college alone, of which Peter is the head, that we believe our Lord entrusted all the blessings of the New Covenant, in order to establish on earth the one Body of Christ into which all those should be fully incorporated who already belong in any way to God's People" (*Decree on Ecumenism*, n. 3).

4. Is it arrogant of the Catholic Church to claim that it is the one, true Church of Jesus Christ?

A. Not if the claim is true. It would not be considered arrogant, for example, to claim that the world is round and not flat, or that George Washington was the first President of the United States, not John Adams. These are facts and there is nothing wrong with asserting them. By the same token, there is nothing wrong with insisting that the Catholic Church is the true Church of Christ, provided that the statement is correct.

5. Can you summarize briefly why Catholics believe their Church was founded by Christ?

A. The Gospels tell us that Jesus founded a Church while he was on earth when he said to Peter, "You are 'Rock,' and on this rock I will build my church" (Matthew 16:18). Jesus indicated that his Church would last forever when he said, "I am with you always, until the end of the world" (Matthew 28:20).

Catholics believe that their Church was founded by Christ because the current leader of the Catholic Church (the Pope) is the historical successor of St. Peter and because the Catholic Church alone possesses in their fullness four signs—one, holy, catholic, and apostolic—that point to the Church of Christ.

(1) Our Lord said that his Church would have unity ("There shall be one flock then, one shepherd"—John 10:16) and this unity in leadership, worship, and belief is most evident in the Catholic Church.

(2) Since Jesus is holy, his Church must be holy in its members, Sacraments, and miracles. The Catholic Church can claim an extraordinary number of saints and martyrs and holy men, women, and children who have faithfully followed the teachings of our Lord. As for Christ's promise that "signs like these will accompany those who have professed their faith . . . the sick upon whom they lay their hands will recover" (Mark 16:17-18), the Catholic Church has from the beginning been blessed with thousands of miraculous cures all over the world.

(3) Jesus indicated that his Church would be catholic, or universal, when he said that it would last "until the end of the world" and when he told the Apostles to spread it to "all the nations" (Matthew 28:19). Only the Catholic Church has existed since the time of Christ and exists everywhere in the world today.

(4) Only the Catholic Church is apostolic in that its bishops can trace their historical succession back to the Apostles, who were the first bishops of Christ's Church, and the bishops of today are teaching the same things that the Apostles taught. For proof of this, compare the Apostles' Creed from the 1st century with the Nicene Creed from the 4th century and the *Credo of the People of God* issued by Pope Paul VI in 1968.

That is why the bishops of Vatican II professed their belief that "this one, true religion subsists in the catholic and apostolic Church" (*Declaration on Religious Freedom*, n. 1).

6. Is mere membership in the Catholic Church a guarantee that a person will be saved?

A. No, it is not. To be saved a Catholic must follow all the teachings of Christ and his Church and must "persevere in charity." If Catholics fail to do these things, said the Fathers of Vatican II, "not only will they not be saved but they will be the more severely judged" (*Constitution on the Church*, n. 14).

7. Does the statement, "Outside the Church there is no salvation," mean that only Catholics can be saved?

A. No. It means that any human being who is a member of the Catholic Church, either in fact or at least in unconscious desire, can go to heaven. For example, a non-Catholic who truly tries to do good and avoid evil, using the graces God gives him, and who sincerely desires to do everything necessary for salvation, in effect desires to be a member of the Catholic Church, which is the sole vehicle of salvation. This person may never have heard of the Catholic Church, or may be completely unaware that his wish to be saved is equivalent to a wish to belong to the Catholic Church. Nevertheless, God accepts this unwitting desire for membership in the Catholic Church as the equivalent of real membership, and thus those apparently outside the Catholic Church can attain eternal salvation.

Projects:

1. List the key points in Articles 8 and 14-16 of Vatican II's *Constitution on the Church*.

2. List the key points in Vatican II's *Decree on Ecumenism*

3. List the key points in Vatican II's *Declaration on the Relationship of the Church to Non-Christian Religions*.

References:

Catechism of the Catholic Church
Catholic Almanac
Drummey, James J. *Catholic Replies*
Hughes, Philip. *A Popular History of the Reformation*
John Paul II, Pope. *Ut Unum Sint*
Keating, Karl. *Catholicism and Fundamentalism*
Nevins, Albert J., M.M. *Answering a Fundamentalist*
_____. *Strangers at Your Door*
Paul VI, Pope. *Ecclesiam Suam*
Pontifical Council for Promoting Christian Unity. *Principles and Norms of Ecumenism*
Surprised by Truth. Edited by Patrick Madrid
Whalen, William. *Faiths for the Few*
_____. *Separated Brethren*
_____. *Strange Gods*

Chapter 15

Getting to Know God

Purpose: The purpose of this chapter is to get acquainted with God by studying his qualities and attributes and by familiarizing ourselves with the doctrine of the Holy Trinity.

Tips for Teachers: We have been dealing until now primarily with those truths of the Catholic Faith which can be arrived at through the use of human reason. With this chapter, we begin a study of some of the truths that we accept on faith because God, "who can neither deceive nor be deceived," has revealed them to us.

Begin the class by discussing the little time that we actually give to God and point out that the key to the happiness and peace that we are seeking in this troubled world is God. We must get to know him if we are to love and serve him. To do this, it is necessary to discuss his qualities. Take the students through each of the attributes, asking first what they mean and then making sure that each one is clearly understood. You can use some of the qualities to bring up matters that puzzle many people, such as predestination or the apparent good fortune that seems to follow bad people, while bad things seem to happen to good people. The questions and answers will be helpful here.

One possible way of illustrating the qualities of God would be to list them in a column and then scramble their definitions in an adjacent column. It might look like this:

___Infinite   A. Can do all things by a mere act of his will

___Eternal   B. Never changes
___Omnipresent   C. Forgives anyone who seeks his forgiveness

___Immutable   D. Has existed from all time
___All-knowing   E. Rewards good and punishes evil

___All-powerful   F. No limit to his perfections
___All-good and merciful G. Is instantaneously and
                            fully aware of everything
___All-just   H. Is present everywhere at
                            the same time

Have the students match up the correct definition with each quality (the answers are F-D-H-B-G-A-C-E).

The second part of the class concerns the most sublime mystery of our Faith—the Blessed Trinity. Start by showing how often we call upon the Trinity without even really thinking about it, e.g., every time we make the Sign of the Cross. Then spend time discussing what the word "mystery" means and ask for examples from everyday life where we accept things on faith or on the word of people we trust.

Next, state the doctrine of the Trinity, stressing that while we can assert what it is, we cannot fully grasp or understand it. It is beyond our human reason. We can know something about the Trinity, but not everything. Explain the difference between person and nature and use the analogies of a shamrock, the lighted candles, and the three forms of water (liquid, ice, steam) to draw a parallel, inadequate though it may be, with the three Persons in one God. Frank Sheed's book, *Theology for Beginners*, particularly chapters 4-6, will be most helpful here.

Lastly, make the point that it is good for us not to know everything, but to have to make an act of faith in God. If we could figure all things out for ourselves, we might forget who gave us our reasoning powers and we might try to set ourselves up as God's equals.

Topics for Discussion:

1. Is it possible for us to really understand ourselves and the world around us without knowing something about God?

2. Choose three qualities of God and explain what they mean.

3. If people fully realized that God knows and sees everything we do, and will one day judge us accordingly, would it stop them from committing evil acts?

4. What do we mean when we say the Trinity is a mystery?

5. Explain the difference between nature and person.

Some Questions and Answers:

1. If God is all-just, why does he let bad people prosper and good people struggle and fail?

A. While God ultimately will reward the good and punish evildoers, he never said it would all be taken care of in this life. The greatest portion of reward and punishment will be meted out after death. It should be remembered that even bad people have some good in them and perhaps receive their little reward in this life; conversely, good people are sinners, too, and may undergo trials and punishment in this life since they are to have eternal happiness in heaven. In any case, we may be sure that God will eventually punish the bad and reward the good, and someday we will understand his plan better than we do now.

2. If God is all-good and all-powerful, why does he permit evil and suffering in the world?

A. The presence of evil and suffering in the world is a mystery that we will not fully understand until the final judgment, but Holy Scripture and the teaching of the Church can shed some light on it. Consider the following points:

(1) God created the first humans in a state of holiness, but Adam and Eve, at the urging of Satan, set themselves against God and brought evil into the world. As a result of their sin, said Vatican II, "men have frequently fallen into multiple errors. . . . The result has been the corruption of morals and human institutions and not rarely contempt for the human person himself" (*Decree on the Apostolate of the Laity*, n. 7). Thus, the evils of the world are traceable not to God but to original sin and the personal sins we commit.

(2) While God is not the cause of evil and suffering, he permits these afflictions in order to draw some good out of them. For instance, out of the suffering and death of Jesus came eternal salvation. If Jesus did not die on the cross, we could not get to heaven.

(3) If we join our sufferings with those of Christ, they will bring us closer to him. Who knows more about homelessness and poverty than our Lord, who was born in a stranger's cave and was buried in a stranger's grave? Who knows more about loneliness than our Lord, who was abandoned by all his friends? Who knows more about injustice than our Lord, who was falsely accused and convicted of a crime though he was innocent? Who knows more about pain than our Lord, who underwent brutal torture and an excruciating death? "Come to me, all you who are weary and find life burdensome," says Jesus, "and I will refresh you" (Matthew 11:28).

(4) In his apostolic letter *On the Christian Meaning of Human Suffering*, Pope John Paul II said that "suffering is present in the world in order to release love, in order to give birth to works of love toward neighbor, in order to transform the whole of human civilization into a 'civilization of love.' " Thus, suffering can be beneficial if it stirs in us a spirit of compassion, love, and sacrifice toward others. The parents of a severely handicapped child, for example, can be an inspiration to others with their love and devotion for their offspring. A person taking care of an old and difficult parent can give a marvelous example of kindness and patience. A person with a terminal illness can offer up their sufferings for sins that he or she committed years before, or for sinners who are on the brink of hell because they have no one to pray for them.

(5) Patient suffering can also prepare us for the life to come. If we suffer with Christ, says St. Paul, we will be "glorified with him. I consider the sufferings of the present to be as nothing compared with the glory to be revealed in us" (Romans 8:17-18).

3. If God is all-knowing, he knows whether I am going to heaven or hell, so there is nothing I can do about it, right?

A. Wrong. You are confusing predestination with God's foreknowledge. Yes, God knows who will be saved and who will be lost, but he does not cause anyone to go to hell. Suppose you have knowledge of the stock market and predict that within six months a certain stock will go up 20 points. And suppose that six months later that stock is indeed up 20 points.

Did you cause the stock to increase in value, or was it just your superior knowledge of market conditions that enabled you to predict this would happen?

No one in hell was predestined there by God. Those in hell deliberately and knowingly committed grave sins and persisted in them until the end of their lives. They freely chose to reject God's Commandments, to resist his grace, and to refuse his love and mercy. It is their fault, not God's, that they are in hell.

God did not want us to be puppets or robots, so he gave us free will. He wants us to choose him freely. He gives us all the grace we need to be saved. He shows love and concern for us even when we turn away from him. He says to the sinner, "Come now, let us set things right. . . . Though your sins be like scarlet, they may become white as snow" (Isaiah 1:18).

God "wants all men to be saved and come to know the truth," says St. Paul (1 Timothy 2:4). God has "predestined us through Christ Jesus to be his adopted sons" (Ephesians 1:5). If we leave ourselves open to God's grace and love, receive his sacraments frequently, and follow the teachings of his Church, then heaven, not hell, will be our final destination.

4. Would it be correct to refer to "God the Mother?"

A. No, it would not be correct. God is a living spirit whom we can come to know by applying the natural light of human reason to the wonders of his creation and by listening to the words of Jesus, the Son of God. When Scripture says that we are made in the image and likeness of God (Genesis 1:26), it means that we have a spirit like his that allows us to think and reason, to choose between right and wrong, and to love. We do not resemble God in our bodies since he does not have a material body.

We call God "Father" not as any affront against mothers or womanhood, but because Jesus told us to call God "our Father." We associate certain qualities with fathers, such as protective love, fidelity, leadership, strength, security, and stability, and Jesus undoubtedly gave us this analogy to help us understand better the nature of God.

Projects:

1. The next time you attend Mass, recite or sing with fervor the words of the Gloria—the great hymn of praise to God. Notice, too, how many references there are to the Father, Son, and Holy Spirit during the course of the Mass.

2. Include as part of your daily prayers this tribute to the Trinity: "Glory be to the Father, and to the Son, and to the Holy Spirit. As it was in the beginning, is now, and ever shall be, world without end. Amen."

3. Recite the prayer given to the children at Fatima by the angel who appeared to them prior to the visitations of the Blessed Mother:

> O most Holy Trinity, Father, Son, and Holy Spirit, I adore you profoundly. I offer you the most precious Body, Blood, Soul, and Divinity of Jesus Christ, present in all the tabernacles of the world, in reparation for the outrages, sacrileges, and indifference by which he is offended. By the infinite merits of the Sacred Heart of Jesus, and the Immaculate Heart of Mary, I beg the conversion of poor sinners.

References:

Catechism of the Catholic Church
Catholic Encyclopedia. Edited by Rev. Peter Stravinskas
Drummey, James J. Catholic Replies
John Paul II, Pope. Dominum et Vivificantem
_____. Salvifici Doloris
Hardon, John. The Catholic Catechism
_____. Modern Catholic Dictionary
_____. The Question and Answer Catholic Catechism
Kreeft, Peter. Fundamentals of the Faith
_____. Making Sense Out of Suffering
Shaw, Russell. Does Suffering Make Sense?
Sheed, Frank. Theology for Beginners
_____. Theology and Sanity
Wuerl, Donald, Lawler, Thomas and Lawler, Ronald. The Catholic Catechism
_____. The Teaching of Christ

Chapter 16

In the Beginning . . .

Purpose: The purpose of this chapter is to provide some insight into the fact and meaning of creation and to stress the tragic effects of original sin on the human race.

Tips for Teachers: Start the class by recalling that when the Apollo 8 spaceship orbited the moon in 1968, the astronauts chose to read from the book of Genesis as their Christmas Eve message to the world. How appropriate it is in this era of space exploration to give some thought to what happened at the beginning.

To familiarize the students with the creation account, have them read aloud from the first three chapters of Genesis (they should have been assigned these chapters for this class). Discuss and explain as you go along the fact and meaning of the creation by God of the visible world and the first human beings. Call attention to the supernatural gifts which Adam and Eve possessed and then lost because of their sins of pride and disobedience, the effects of original sin on the human race, and God's promise of a Redeemer who would atone for the sin of Adam. The material under questions and answers will be helpful.

Make sure that the students understand clearly that the Bible is religious history and not a scientific explanation of the origin of the universe. But also point out that the Genesis account, like everything else in the Bible, "must be acknowledged as teaching firmly, faithfully, and without error that truth which God wanted put into the sacred writings for the sake of our salvation" (Vatican II, *Constitution on Divine Revelation*, n. 11).

Spend some time on the good and bad angels (devils) and how they can influence our lives. These spiritual beings are very much a part of our world and we should not ignore them.

Topics for Discussion:

1. Why did God create the world and human beings?

2. What are angels? What happened after God created them? (See 2 Peter 2:4 and Jude 1:6).

3. What special gifts did Adam and Eve possess before they sinned?

4. How does original sin affect us?

5. Why are there so many books, articles, and films about the devil?

6. Comment on the statement, "A person who denies the existence of the devil offers the clearest proof that he does exist."

7. Is it a good philosophy of life to do "our own thing," or should we try to do "God's thing"?

Some Questions and Answers:

1. If God is a spirit, how can we be created in his image and likeness?

A. When we say that we are created in the image and likeness of God, we are not referring to our bodies, since God does not have a body, but rather to our souls, which, like God, are spirits possessing intelligence and free will.

2. What is the soul? Can we prove that we have one?

A. The soul is not a physical part of the body or anything tangible. It is the principle of life, the principle of such spiritual activities as thinking and willing. We know that we have a soul because we can understand and want abstract and non-material things, such as honor, goodness, and justice. Such understanding and wanting would be impossible if we were made up exclusively of matter.

3. As Catholics, are we supposed to believe the story of the creation of the world and of Adam and Eve and how God punished them for eating an apple?

A. The story of creation and of Adam and Eve is one of the most beautiful and inspiring passages in all of literature. In answering the question, we might consider these points:

(1) The book of Genesis was not intended to be a scientific and anthropological treatise of the origins of the universe and the human race. The author was not trying to teach exactly how the world was created, but rather the fact and meaning of creation. Thus, Genesis is a book of religious history in which the author used figurative language and popular descriptions to teach people fundamental religious truths concerning their salvation.

(2) Some of these fundamental religious truths are: that God in his goodness created the universe out of nothing; that everything he created was good; that he created the first humans in his image and likeness; that marriage is the union of man and woman; that the first man lost his state of perfect happiness through the sins of pride and disobedience; that the whole human race suffers from the consequences of Adam's sin; and that one day there will be a Redeemer for fallen humanity.

(3) The story of Adam and Eve is not a myth or a highly imaginary tale. There were first parents from whom the entire human race is descended. They are called Adam because the Hebrew word for "man" is adam, and Eve, who became the mother of all the living, because her name is related to the Hebrew word for "living."

(4) Catholics are not expected to accept the Bible's description of the creation of Adam from clay and Eve from Adam's rib as scientifically precise and literally true, although God could have created them in this fashion. The symbolic language is used to signify Adam's nearness and likeness to God and his dominion over all other created things. The description of Eve being made from Adam's rib shows that woman is equal in dignity to man and is meant to be at man's side as a companion through all the joys and sorrows of life.

(5) The sin of Adam and Eve was not the eating of the apple; there is no mention of an apple in Genesis, in fact. Their sin was not even eating the fruit of the tree of knowledge of good and evil. Rather, it was the essence of all sin—rebellion against God. In their pride and their desire to be equal to God, they succumbed to the temptation of Satan and disobeyed God. Like the fallen angels, who also rebelled against God, Adam and Eve suffered disastrous consequences. But unlike the bad

angels, God gave them a second chance by promising to send a Redeemer (Genesis 3:15).

(6) The sin of Adam and Eve, called original sin because we inherit it by our origin, or descent, from our first parents, means that every member of the human race is born in sin, is subject to death and suffering, has a strong inclination toward evil, and has no right to heaven until he or she has been baptized. The doctrine of original sin was infallibly defined by the Council of Trent and has been affirmed by Vatican II, recent Popes, and the *Catechism of the Catholic Church.*

4. How do we know there are spirits known as angels?

A. We know that angels exist from the Bible and from the word of the infallible Church of Christ. There are numerous references to angels throughout the Old Testament and the New Testament. For example, angels played a role in the events surrounding the birth of Jesus (Matthew 1:20-24; Luke 1:26-38, 2:9-15), his temptation in the desert (Matthew 4:11), his agony in the garden (Luke 22:43), his resurrection (Matthew 28:2-7; Mark 16:5-7; Luke 24:4-7; John 20:12-13), and his ascension into heaven (Acts 1:10-11).

Also, the Fourth Lateran Council in 1215 infallibly defined the existence of angels, and Pope Paul VI, in his *Credo of the People of God*, declared that God created "things invisible such as the pure spirits which are called angels." (Cf. *Catechism of the Catholic Church*, nn. 328-336).

5. Is it true that every person has a Guardian Angel assigned to watch over us?

A. Yes. The doctrine of guardian angels, although not explicitly defined as a matter of faith, is firmly grounded in Church tradition. It is based on the words of Christ when he warned against scandalizing little children: "See that you never despise one of these little ones. I assure you, their angels in heaven constantly behold my heavenly Father's face" (Matthew 18:10).

In the Old Testament, God told Moses, "I am sending an angel before you, to guard you on the way and bring you to the place I have prepared. Be attentive to him and heed his voice. Do not rebel against him, for he will not forgive your sin. My authority resides in him" (Exodus 23:20-21).

St. Thomas Aquinas explained the doctrine this way: "Man while in this state of life is, as it were, on a road by which he should journey towards heaven. On this road man is threatened by many dangers both from within and without . . . and therefore as guardians are appointed for men who have to pass by an unsafe road, so an angel guardian is assigned to each man as long as he is a wayfarer."

Projects:

1. Read the first three chapters of Genesis and list some of the religious truths found there.

2. Look at daily newspaper and clip five stories which illustrate the effects of original sin on the modern world.

3. Attend a baptismal instruction the next time one is held in your parish, or act out the rite of Baptism in class.

4. List three scriptural references where angels played an important part in the life of Christ.

References:

Anderson, Joan Wester. *An Angel to Watch Over Me*
_____. *Where Angels Walk*
Balducci, Corrado. *The Devil . . . Alive and Active in Our World*
Catechism of the Catholic Church
Cristiani, Msgr. Leon. *Satan in the Modern World*
Drummey, James J. *Catholic Replies*
Hardon, John. *The Catholic Catechism*
_____. *Modern Catholic Dictionary*
_____. *The Question and Answer Catholic Catechism*
John Paul II, Pope. *Reconciliation and Penance*
Kreeft, Peter. *Angels and Demons*
Pius XII, Pope. *Humani Generis*
Ratzinger, Joseph Cardinal. *In the Beginning*
Sacred Congregation for Divine Worship. *Christian Faith and Demonology*
Steffon, Rev. Jeffrey J. *Satanism: Is It Real?*

Chapter 17

The World's Greatest Evil

Purpose: The purpose of this chapter is to give the students a disgust for sin and a firm resolve to remain in the state of grace.

Tips for Teachers: Begin by asking the class what it thinks is the greatest evil in the world today. Write the answers on the board and show how sin is at the root of all the evils listed. Seek examples to prove that our society has lost its sense of sin.

Establish a definition of sin and discuss the different kinds of sin, why a mortal sin is such a grave offense, the conditions for a mortal sin, the danger of venial sin, temptations and their origin, and occasions of sin. Use the board as much as possible and try to involve the students as much as possible.

Finally, discuss the seven capital sins as the root of all other sins. You could list them in one column on a paper and scramble their definitions in another column as we did with the qualities of God in chapter 15.

It is not fashionable today to talk about sin and hell. Do not let this deter you. Lack of awareness and concern for these matters is part of the reason why sin and evil are rampant in the world. To ignore or play down these realities is a disservice to God and to your students. For a good summary of sin and specific examples of right and wrong, see *Sharing the Light of Faith*, pages 55-61, and *Veritatis Splendor*, nn. 13, 49, 80, 81, 100, and 101.

Topics for Discussion:

1. What is the greatest evil of our time?
2. Give examples of current books, magazines, movies, and television programs which indicate that our society has lost its sense of sin.
3. What is sin and how many kinds of sin are there?

4. Explain the meaning of the saying, "A saint is a sinner who kept on trying."

5. What is an occasion of sin?

Some Questions and Answers:

1. If God is good and merciful, why would he send a person to hell for just one mortal sin?

A. Yes, God is merciful, but he is also just. He rewards good and punishes evil. Because of one serious sin, God created hell and cast the bad angels into it forever. Because of one serious sin, God cast Adam and Eve from Paradise, thus subjecting them and all their descendants to pain, sickness, and death. Sin is such a grave offense against a loving and just God that it deserves grave punishment.

But we have the consolation of knowing that no matter what grave sins we commit, God is always willing to forgive us if we are truly sorry. Those persons in hell sent themselves there by stubbornly persisting in their sins and by refusing to seek God's mercy and forgiveness.

2. Why is mortal sin such a grave offense?

A. First, it takes away sanctifying grace, thus killing God's life in our soul. Second, it makes us an enemy of God and takes away our right to heaven. Third, it deprives us of all reward for our good actions and exposes us to the danger of everlasting punishment in hell.

3. What are the three conditions for a mortal sin?

A. First, the thought, desire, word, deed, or omission must be a serious violation of the law of God or of the Church. Second, the person must know that it is a serious violation. Third, the person must willfully and deliberately carry out the grave violation. All three conditions must be present for a sin to be mortal. If one condition is lacking, the sin is venial.

4. What is a temptation? Are temptations sinful?

A. A temptation is an invitation to commit a sin arising from the allurements of the world, the desires of the flesh, or the urgings of the devil. God allows us to be tempted and gives us the grace to fight off temptations. Temptations themselves are never sinful, no matter how strong they are or how long they last. Sin occurs only when we give in to the temptations.

5. What is an exorcism?

A. An exorcism, says the *Catholic Almanac*, is a ritual of the Catholic Church in which evil spirits are charged and commanded on the authority of God and with the prayer of the Church to depart from a person or to cease causing harm to a person suffering from diabolical possession or obsession. The sacramental is officially administered by a priest delegated for the purpose by the bishop of the place. Elements of the rite include the Litany of the Saints; recitation of the Our Father and one or more creeds; specific prayers of exorcism; reading of Gospel passages; and use of the Sign of the Cross.

Exorcisms are still performed today when there is clear evidence of the presence of devils. One priest, who performed exorcisms in Rome for more than twenty-five years, said that "it is a terrible strain, both physically and mentally." He said that the possessing demons use such "unbelievably obscene" language that "you have to steel yourself and remember that the Church is behind you, although I have been afraid on occasion."

Projects:

1. Read again the account of the Passion in chapter 7 to see what our sins did to Christ.

2. Go to Confession at least once a month, even if you have not committed a mortal sin, to get the grace you need to avoid sin.

3. Set a good example for others by refusing to do something sinful just because "everyone else is doing it."

4. Say every day the prayer to St. Michael the Archangel that appears on pages 194-195.

References:

Catechism of the Catholic Church
Dilenno, Dr. Joseph, and Smith, Herbert, S.J. *Homosexuality: The Questions*

Drummey, James J. *Catholic Replies*
Fox, Rev. Robert J. *The Gift of Sexuality*
Grisez, Germain. *Christian Moral Principles*
_____. *Living a Christian Life*
Hardon, John. *The Catholic Catechism*
_____. *The Question and Answer Catholic Catechism*
Harvey, John. *The Homosexual Person*
John Paul II, Pope. *Evangelium Vitae*
_____. *Reconciliation and Penance*
_____. *Veritatis Splendor*
Jone, Heribert, O.F.M. Cap., *Moral Theology*
Kippley, John. *Sex and the Marriage Covenant*
Lawler, Ronald, Boyle, Joseph and May, William. *Catholic Sexual Ethics*
May, William. *An Introduction to Moral Theology*
Pontifical Council for the Family. *The Truth and Meaning of Human Sexuality*
Sacred Congregation for Divine Worship. *Christian Faith and Demonology*
Sacred Congregation for the Doctrine of the Faith. *Declaration on Certain Problems of Sexual Ethics*
Stravinskas, Rev. Peter M.J. *The Catholic Answer Book*
_____. *The Catholic Answer Book 2*
Thayer, Linda. *AIDS & Adolescents*
U.S. Bishops. *Sharing the Light of Faith*
Wuerl, Donald, Lawler, Thomas and Lawler, Ronald. *The Catholic Catechism*
_____. *The Teaching of Christ*

Chapter 18

Jesus Christ—God and Man

Purpose: The purpose of this chapter is to give the students a clear understanding and deep appreciation of the two greatest events in all human history—the Incarnation and the Redemption.

Tips for Teachers: Begin by reviewing the Old Testament prophecies concerning the Messiah and show how they were fulfilled in Jesus. Then go over the Gospel accounts of the Annunciation and the Nativity, leading into a discussion of why Jesus became man and why he chose to be born in a cave in the village of Bethlehem. While discussing the Incarnation, explain the doctrine of Jesus' two natures in one person, mentioning again, as we did in chapter 15, the difference between a nature and a person. This doctrine has led to some of the most serious heresies in the Church, and our own generation has not been immune to them.

The second part of the class should focus on the Redemption, whereby the Second Person of the Blessed Trinity became one of us and suffered and died a horrible death to make reparation for our sins. Jesus came down to earth so that we could be taken up to heaven. Try to stress the stupendous significance of this example of "love par exellence," and emphasize the tremendous debt of gratitude we owe to God and the absolute necessity on our part of renouncing sin and always trying to stay close to him.

Finally, discuss the descent of Christ to the Limbo of the Fathers, his resurrection from the dead, and his ascension into heaven, where he sits at the right hand of God until he comes again in glory to judge the living and the dead at the end of the world.

Topics for Discussion:

1. Has the title "Prince of Peace" ever been associated

with any worldly ruler? Who was the first person to use this title to describe Jesus?

2. Why did Jesus choose to be born in a stable instead of a palace or at least a house?

3. What do we mean by the Incarnation? The Redemption? The Ascension?

4. What does Jesus' death and resurrection mean to you?

Some Questions and Answers:

1. Why was the Incarnation necessary?

A. The Incarnation was necessary because Adam and Eve had committed an infinite offense against God. No mere human being could make up for that offense. The people of the Old Testament tried to do so through sacrifices of animals and crops, but they were unsuccessful. It was only when God, the Second Person of the Blessed Trinity, took on a human nature that atonement for the sin of Adam was possible. As God, Jesus could offer infinite reparation to his Father for the offense; as man, he could take the place of sinful humanity and do penance for our sins.

2. Was Jesus actually born on December 25th?

A. The actual date of our Lord's birth is not known. By the fourth century, however, the Church was celebrating the Nativity on December 25th. It is thought that the Church chose this particular date to offset a major holiday for the pagan Romans, the commemoration of the birth of the sun at the winter solstice.

3. What do we mean by the hypostatic union?

A. This is the theological term used to indicate that the two distinct natures of Christ (human and divine) are united in the one Person of Jesus.

4. Has the doctrine of the two natures in the one person of Jesus ever been disputed?

A. It certainly has. Many major heresies have arisen that denied at least one aspect of this doctrine. In the first eight centuries of the Church, for example, there was Arianism, which denied the divinity of Christ and regarded him only as a superior creature and the intermediary between God and the world; Nestorianism, which denied the real union of the divine and human natures in Christ and taught that while Mary could be called the Mother of Christ as man, she could not be called the Mother of God; and Subordinationism and Adoptionism, which taught that Christ was subordinate to God, that he was the Son of God not by nature but by adoption.

Even in our own day, there are some in the Catholic Church who question the divinity of Christ. Recognizing this problem, the Vatican's Sacred Congregation for the Doctrine of the Faith released in 1972 *Mysterium Filii Dei*, its declaration on "Errors Concerning the Mysteries of the Incarnation and the Trinity." The declaration said that those who view Jesus merely as a divinely inspired human being "are far removed from true belief in Christ, even when they maintain that the special presence of God in Jesus results in his being the supreme and final expression of Divine Revelation."

5. What do we mean when we say that Jesus descended into hell, or that he descended to the dead?
A. By this we mean that Jesus, after his death on the cross, went to the abode of the dead or "lower regions" of the earth, which is *sheol* in Hebrew and *hades* in Greek. It was to this place, also known as the Limbo of the Fathers, that Jesus "went to preach to the spirits in prison" (1 Peter 3:19). He went there to free the souls of the just men and women who had died before his redeeming death on the cross and to take them to heaven.

Projects:

1. Refer back to chapter 6 and list the prophecies from the Old Testament pertaining to the birth of Jesus.

2. Read the Gospel accounts of the Nativity and the events surrounding it and write a newspaper story based on the accounts

3. Look up in a history of the Church or in a *Catholic Encyclopedia* the heresy of Arianism and write a paper showing the chaos it caused in the second and third centuries.

4. Read the Apostles' Creed or the Nicene Creed and list

the doctrines in each statement of beliefs that have to do with Jesus.

References:

Catechism of the Catholic Church
Daniel-Rops, Henri. *Jesus and His Times* (2 vols.)
Drummey, James J. *Catholic Replies*
Hardon, John. *The Catholic Catechism*
_____. *Modern Catholic Dictionary*
_____. *The Question and Answer Catholic Catechism*
Hughes, Philip. *A Popular History of the Catholic Church*
Kreeft, Peter. *Letters to Jesus (Answered)*
_____. and Tacelli, Ronald K. *Handbook of Christian Apologetics*
Most, William. *Catholic Apologetics Today*
_____. *The Consciousness of Christ.*
Nevins, Albert J., M.M. *Catholicism: The Faith of Our Fathers*
Ricciotti, Giuseppe. *The Life of Christ*
Sheed, Frank. *To Know Christ Jesus*
_____. *What Difference Does Jesus Make?*
Sheen, Fulton J. *Life of Christ*
Wuerl, Donald, Lawler, Thomas and Lawler, Ronald. *The Catholic Catechism*
_____. *The Teaching of Christ*

Chapter 19

Grace and the Virtues

Purpose: The purpose of this chapter is to show the supernatural helps that God has made available to us, both to aid us in this life and to insure that we will share an eternity of happiness with him.

Tips for Teachers: This class involves a lot of terms and definitions, so use the board as much as possible.

Begin by discussing whether the Catholic Church keeps us from enjoying ourselves, drawing the distinction between the fleeting pleasures in this life and an eternity of joy and happiness with God. Take up the questions of "Who am I?" and "Why am I here?" The answers to these questions will help set the stage for a discussion of grace—what it is, how many kinds there are, the difference between them, and why grace is necessary for us. Make sure to encourage the students to frequent the Sacraments and to pray all the time, using some of the prayers we have suggested or others of their own choosing.

Conclude with a discussion of the theological and moral virtues and the gifts of the Holy Spirit, explaining each of them and emphasizing whichever ones seem pertinent at the time. In these days of confusion and uncertainty, for example, a brief discussion of the virtue of hope—putting all our trust in God— might be appropriate.

Topics for Discussion:

1. Does the Catholic Church take all the fun out of life?
2. List and explain the four kinds of life.
3. What is grace and how many kinds of grace are there?
4. Describe the three theological virtues.
5. Explain the seven gifts of the Holy Spirit.
6. What are the four cardinal virtues?

Some Questions and Answers:

1. Who are we and why are we here on earth?

A. We are human beings with material bodies and spiritual souls. Because God's love was so great that he wanted to share his happiness with us, he gave us a super-nature as well as a human nature. This super-nature, which we call sanctifying grace, enables us to share in the life of God.

Why are we here? We are here to love God and to love our neighbor. We were created to know, love, and serve God in this world so that we might be happy with him forever in the next world.

2. What is the difference between actual grace and sanctifying grace?

A. Actual grace is a special supernatural help from God which enlightens our minds and strengthens our wills to do good and to avoid evil. It is a passing, fleeting, temporary grace by which God speaks to us and inspires us to do the right thing at a certain time. This grace can be ignored or rejected. Actual graces can be persons (a priest, religious, or some holy layperson), places (a church), or things (a newspaper ad or television commercial that mentions God) that remind us of our obligation to serve God.

Sanctifying grace is intended to be a permanent, lasting quality in our souls. It raises our human nature to a supernatural level and enables us to share in the divine life of God. It remains in our soul until we commit a mortal sin and can only be restored through contrition and confession of our sins in the sacrament of Penance/Reconciliation. Absolutely essential for us to get to heaven, sanctifying grace may be increased by prayer and the sacraments.

3. Is grace really necessary for us?

A. Yes. Without the supernatural help of God, our weak human nature would not be able to resist evil. Furthermore, we need divine assistance to rise above our natures and to share in the divine life of God. We cannot attain salvation by our own natural efforts.

Projects:

1. Compose a prayer of your own and say it every day.

2. Make the Acts of Faith, Hope, and Charity a part of your daily prayer-life

3. List some ways of Christian living that might make you an actual grace for persons who are away from God and his Church.

4. Ask the Holy Spirit to give you the gifts of wisdom and fortitude so you can be an effective witness to Christ.

References:

Catechism of the Catholic Church
Catholic Encyclopedia. Edited by Rev. Peter Stravinskas
Drummey, James J. *Catholic Replies*
Halligan, Nicholas, O.P. *The Sacraments and Their Celebration*
Hardon, John. *The Catholic Catechism*
_____. *Modern Catholic Dictionary*
_____. *The Question and Answer Catholic Catechism*
Kreeft, Peter. *Fundamentals of the Faith*
_____. and Tacelli, Ronald K. *Handbook of Christian Apologetics*
Sheed, Frank. *Theology for Beginners*
Wuerl, Donald, Lawler, Thomas and Lawler, Ronald. *The Catholic Catechism*
_____. *The Teaching of Christ*

Chapter 20

The Bridge to Eternity

Purpose: The purpose of this chapter is to show the common spiritual bond that exists among all members of the Mystical Body of Christ, and also to demonstrate the value of frequent Confession as a remedy for sin.

Tips for Teachers: Begin this class by using the first or second discussion question and then lead into a discussion of the Mystical Body—what it is, what our relationship should be with Christ and our brothers and sisters, and how we can help each other, both spiritually and materially. Spend some time on the spiritual and corporal works of mercy, explaining how each one is applicable to us and encouraging the students to perform them on a regular basis.

Next, discuss the doctrine of the Communion of Saints, emphasizing the link we have with the saints in heaven and the souls in purgatory and the necessity of prayers to those in heaven and for those in purgatory.

Finally, take up the doctrine of the forgiveness of sins. Note the origins of the sacrament of Penance/Reconciliation, the source of grace that it offers, and the value of frequent Confession. Using the material under questions and answers, state the Church's clear and unchanging position on Penance. Be very positive about it, for if the students do not hear the teaching of the Church from you, there is the possibility that they may not hear it at all.

Topics for Discussion:

1. Explain the meaning of the statement, "The good or evil done to another is good or evil done to Christ."

2. If the Church were a baseball team, would your actions be raising or lowering its batting average?

3. What are the seven corporal works of mercy? Which

ones can you perform most frequently?

4. What are the seven spiritual works of mercy? Which ones can you perform most frequently?

5. What do we mean by the Communion of Saints?

6. How do we know that a priest has the power to forgive sins?

Some Questions and Answers:

1. What do we mean by the Mystical Body of Christ?

A. The Mystical Body of Christ refers to the Church of which Christ is the head, the Holy Spirit the soul, and the faithful, living and dead, the members. The doctrine, which stems from Christ's statement, "I am the vine, you are the branches" (John 15:5), describes the real and spiritual union which the faithful have with Christ and with their brothers and sisters.

"By communicating his Spirit to his brothers, called together from all peoples, Christ made them mystically into his own body," said the Second Vatican Council. "In that body, the life of Christ is poured into the believers, who, through the sacraments, are united in a hidden and real way to Christ who suffered and was glorified" (*Constitution on the Church*, n. 7). The Council said that this unity, sustained by the Holy Eucharist, is such that "if one member suffers anything, all the members suffer it too, and if one member is honored, all the members rejoice together (cf. 1 Corinthians 12:26)."

2. Why do Catholics pray to the saints? Why not pray directly to God?

A. Many Catholics do pray directly to God and that's fine, But there is nothing wrong with praying to the saints and asking them to intercede for us with God. The saints once experienced the same problems and temptations we face and they overcame them with lives of great holiness. They give us a good example to follow and we take their names at Baptism and Confirmation so that they will help us in our daily lives.

A person seeking a job could go directly to the head of the company. Or he or she could ask a friend to speak to the boss first. Either approach is perfectly acceptable in this situation or in our relationship with God and the saints. Just as it can be beneficial to have a friend who knows the head of the company, so also it can be helpful to have friends in heaven who can speak to God on our behalf.

3. Does the Church still require that we receive the sacrament of Penance/Reconciliation at least once a year? Do we have to go to Confession if we have committed only venial sins?

A. It is one of the commandments or precepts of the Church that Catholics must receive the sacrament of Penance or Reconciliation at least once a year if they have committed a mortal sin. But if the person is not conscious of having committed a mortal sin, then annual Confession is not mandatory. Canon 989 of the Code of Canon Law makes this clear by saying that "after having attained the age of discretion, each of the faithful is bound by an obligation faithfully to confess serious sins at least once a year."

As for venial sins, Pope John Paul II said, "Though the Church knows and teaches that venial sins are forgiven in other ways too—for instance, by acts of sorrow, works of charity, prayer, penitential rites—she does not cease to remind everyone of the special usefulness of the sacramental moment for these sins too. The frequent use of the sacrament . . . strengthens the awareness that even minor sins offend God and harm the Church, the Body of Christ" (*Reconciliation and Penance*, n. 32).

4. Why do we confess our sins to a priest? Why not confess them directly to God?

A. There are several reasons. First, because that is what Jesus wants us to do. On Easter Sunday night, our Lord told the Apostles, his first priests, "Receive the Holy Spirit. If you forgive men's sins, they are forgiven them; if you hold them bound, they are held bound" (John 20:22-23). Since "hold them bound" means not to forgive them, the Apostles could not know what sins to forgive or not forgive unless they were first told the sins by the penitent.

Second, telling our sins to a priest teaches us humility, something we could not learn if we confessed our sins privately to God. Third, we receive graces from the sacrament of Penance. Fourth, by absolving us of our sins, the priest, who is representing Christ, gives us the assurance that our sins have been forgiven. And fifth, the priest can give us some sound advice on how to avoid sin in the future, while the person praying in private receives no helpful instructions.

In his statement on *Reconciliation and Penance*, Pope John Paul urged Catholics to confess their sins often to a priest, saying that it would be "foolish . . . to disregard the means of grace and salvation which the Lord has provided and . . . to claim to receive forgiveness while doing without the sacrament which was instituted by Christ precisely for forgiveness" (n. 31).

5. In some parishes, you can go to a Penance service and receive general absolution, with no private confession of sins. Is that all right to do?

A. No, it is not. "Individual and integral Confession and absolution constitute the only ordinary way by which the faithful person who is aware of serious sin is reconciled with God and with the Church," says Canon 960 of the Code of Canon Law. Canon 961 says that general absolution can be given only in cases of grave necessity, such as when "the danger of death is imminent and there is not time for the priest or priests to hear the Confession of individual penitents" (e.g., soldiers going into battle), or when "in the light of the number of penitents a supply of confessors is not readily available rightly to hear the Confessions of individuals within a suitable time so that the penitents are forced to be deprived of sacramental grace or Holy Communion for a long time through no fault of their own."

If the diocesan bishop decides that either of these conditions is present and gives permission for general absolution, the priest must instruct the penitents to be sorry for their sins, to make an Act of Contrition prior to the general absolution, and to have the intention to confess their sins privately to a priest "as soon as there is an opportunity to do so before receiving another general absolution unless a just cause intervenes" (Canon 963).

6. What is an indulgence and how can one be gained?

A. An indulgence is a remission of the temporal punishment due to sins which have already been forgiven. The indulgence can be plenary, which means all temporal punishment is taken away, or only partial, and it can be applied only to the person who performs the indulgenced work or to a soul in purgatory. The previous practice of attaching a certain number of days or years to a specific task is no longer in effect.

According to Pope Paul VI's *Apostolic Constitution on the Revision of Indulgences*, the conditions for gaining a plenary indulgence are: the person must be free from all attachment to sin, even venial sin; must perform the indulgenced work as perfectly as possible; and, within several days before or after doing so, must receive sacramental Confession and Eucharistic Communion, and offer prayers for the intentions of the Holy Father. One Our Father and one Hail Mary would satisfy the latter requirement. If each of these conditions is not fulfilled, the indulgence gained will be only partial.

The number of indulgenced works and prayers was reduced by Pope Paul to about seventy in his *Enchiridion Indulgentiarum*. They consist of acts of charity for those in need, as well as traditional and devotional prayers.

Projects:

1. Perform a work of mercy every week.
2. Go to Confession at least once a month and bring a family member or friend along with you.
3. Write a report on Pope John Paul's apostolic exhortation on *Reconciliation and Penance*.

References:

Catechism of the Catholic Church
John Paul II, Pope. *Reconciliation and Penance*
_____. *Veritatis Splendor*
Pius XII, Pope. *The Mystical Body*
Shaw, Russell. *Why We Need Confession*
Sheed, Frank. *Theology for Beginners*
_____. *Theology and Sanity*

Chapter 21

After Death—What?

Purpose: The purpose of this chapter is to show both the divine origin and the reasonableness of the doctrines of heaven, hell, and purgatory and the absolute necessity of always being prepared for death by remaining in the state of grace.

Tips for Teachers: Begin by discussing whether there is such a thing as life after death, eventually leading into the doctrines of the resurrection of the body, the particular and general judgments, and the existence of heaven, hell, and purgatory. Spend some time on each doctrine, stressing both the logic of the doctrine and the scriptural evidence to support it. Peter Kreeft's book, *Everything You Ever Wanted to Know About Heaven*, which also deals with hell and purgatory, will be very helpful, as will the other sources listed under references.

The visions of hell given to St. Teresa and the children at Fatima can help to enliven any discussion of hell. Give the students some opportunity to present their thoughts on hell, as well as on heaven and purgatory, before you sum up the teaching of the Church. It is not fashionable to talk about hell these days, but the catechist's job is to present the teaching of the Church clearly and unequivocally.

In discussing purgatory, encourage the students to pray for those souls waiting to go to heaven. Not only is it a holy and pious thing for them to do, but, from a practical point of view, there will be fewer people to pray for us when we're in purgatory unless we encourage others to adopt this practice.

Topics for Discussion:

1. Is there a life after death?
2. Why should we always be prepared for death?
3. What do we mean by the resurrection of the body?
4. When Pope Paul, in the *Credo of the People of God*,

referred to hell as "the fire that is not extinguished," what did he mean?

5. What will heaven be like?

Some Questions and Answers:

1. If our fate is already determined at the particular judgment, why will there be a general judgment?

A. When the general judgment takes place at the end of the world, all members of the human race will be judged on how they responded to those in need—the hungry, the thirsty, the sick, the imprisoned. This social judgment will not change the verdict given at the particular judgment, but it will reveal to the whole world God's mercy toward those who are saved and his justice toward those who are condemned.

2. Has anyone besides St. Teresa been given a vision of hell?

A. Yes, the three shepherd children in Fatima were given such a vision when the Blessed Mother visited their Portuguese village on July 13, 1917. In that apparition, our Lady showed them a horrifying sight that one of the seers, Lucia, described some years later as "a sea of fire. Plunged in this fire were demons and souls in human form . . . floating about in the conflagration . . . and shrieks and groans of pain and despair, which horrified us and made us tremble with fear. The demons could be distinguished by their terrifying and repellent likeness to frightful and unknown animals, black and transparent like burning coals."

"You have seen hell where the souls of poor sinners go," the Blessed Virgin told the children. "In order to save them, God wishes to establish in the world devotion to my Immaculate Heart. When you pray the rosary, say after each mystery, 'O my Jesus, forgive us our sins; save us from the fire of hell. Lead all souls to heaven, especially those in most need of your mercy.'"

3. Why do we believe in purgatory when it is not mentioned in the Bible?

A. It is true that the word "purgatory" does not appear

in the Bible. Neither does the word "Trinity," but that doctrine is clearly taught in the Scriptures. And so is the doctrine of prayers for the dead. The second book of Maccabees, which Protestants dropped from their Bible in the 16th century, says that "it is therefore a holy and wholesome thought to pray for the dead, that they may be loosed from their sins" (2 Maccabees 12:46). Since prayers are not needed by those in heaven, and they cannot help those in hell, there must be a third place where people can be helped by prayers.

St. Peter may have been referring to purgatory when he said that after Jesus died, "he went to preach to the spirits in prison" (1 Peter 3:19).

4. Does the Church still believe in Limbo for babies who die without being baptized?

A. The Catholic Church has never made an official pronouncement about Limbo. It does teach that Baptism in some form is required for us to get to heaven. This raises the delicate question of what happens to infants, as well as aborted babies, who die before being baptized. One explanation given by theologians since the 13th century is that these babies go to a place called Limbo, where they enjoy full natural happiness but never experience the Beatific Vision. More recently, the *Catechism of the Catholic Church* (n. 1261) said that "Jesus' tenderness toward children which caused him to say: 'Let the children come to me, do not hinder them,' allow us to hope that there is a way of salvation for children who have died without Baptism."

In the funeral Mass for an unbaptized child, the Church confidently commends these babies to a loving and merciful God with this prayer: "Father of all consolation, from whom nothing is hidden, you know the faith of these parents who mourn the death of their child. May they find comfort in knowing that he/she is entrusted to your loving care."

5. Is the doctrine of purgatory reasonable?

A. It is reasonable because most people have not led such evil or sinful lives as to deserve punishment in hell. At the same time, most people have not led such holy or virtuous lives as to merit immediate entry into heaven. Hence, there must be an intermediate state where those whose souls are stained with venial sins or temporal penalties remaining from forgiven mortal sins can purify themselves before being admitted into heaven. "Purgatory is like heaven's bathroom," says Peter Kreeft, "where you get washed before dinner."

6. What is the Beatific Vision?

A. It is an act of understanding by which the blessed in heaven know God, clearly, directly, and immediately, in himself, his Trinity, and all his attributes. In other words, it means seeing God face to face, as he is, in all his glory.

Projects:

1. Make an act of perfect contrition before going to sleep every night.

2. When you say the Hail Mary, think about the words, "pray for us sinners now and at the hour of our death."

3. When you read or hear of someone who has died, say this prayer: "May their soul and the souls of all the faithful departed, through the mercy of God, rest in peace. Amen."

4. Read chapter 25, verses 31-46, of Matthew's Gospel to get a clear picture of the final judgment.

References:

Catechism of the Catholic Church
Drummey, James J. Catholic Replies
Hardon, John A., S.J. The Catholic Catechism
_____. Modern Catholic Dictionary
_____. The Question and Answer Catholic Catechism
Kreeft, Peter. Everything You Ever Wanted to Know About Heaven
Nevins, Albert J., M.M. Catholicism: The Faith of Our Fathers
Sheed, Frank. Theology for Beginners
_____. Theology and Sanity
Wuerl, Donald, Lawler, Thomas and Lawler, Ronald. The Catholic Catechism
_____. The Teaching of Christ

Chapter 22

Mary, Mother of the Church

Purpose: The purpose of this chapter is to make clear the role of the Blessed Virgin Mary in the Church and in our lives and to encourage devotion to her.

Tips for Teachers: The catechist may begin by using the story about Oberammergau or by asking the students if devotion to the Blessed Mother has any value today. This could lead to a discussion of Vatican's II's high regard for Mary and the three reasons why we should turn to her for help. Spend enough time on the Immaculate Conception and the Virgin Birth to make sure that both are clear to the students. Use the miracle at Cana to show how Jesus responded to a request from his mother.

The students will be especially interested in the apparitions of the Blessed Virgin. Have them research one or more of them and present a report to the class. The appearances at Fatima in 1917 are particularly fascinating because of the startling predictions that were made—some of which have since come true.

The introduction to *A Woman Clothed With the Sun*, by John Delaney, provides a superb summary of eight apparitions and includes the striking similarities common to all of them—the people and places involved, Mary's physical appearance, the phenomena accompanying her appearances, and her message. This summary is must reading.

The teacher might also consider reading to the students William Thomas Walsh's powerful description of the violent storm which blasted Portugal on October 12, 1917, the night before the Miracle of the Sun. This description can be found both in Walsh's own book, *Our Lady of Fatima*, and in *A Woman Clothed With the Sun*.

Finally, discuss the great spiritual value of the rosary, mentioning its role in history, the enthusiasm which Popes have had for it, and the proper way of reciting it. A candlelight rosary procession would be a very worthwhile project, especially on one of Mary's feast days. A scriptural rosary, with an appropriate verse or two from the Bible after each Hail Mary, is also very effective.

Topics for Discussion:

1. Did the Second Vatican Council downgrade the role of the Blessed Mother and discourage devotion to her?

2. Give three reasons why Catholics should turn to Mary.

3. What do we mean by the Immaculate Conception? How does it differ from the Virgin Birth?

4. Why do you think the Blessed Mother has appeared primarily to children and in remote areas of the world?

5. Why is the rosary such an important devotion?

Some Questions and Answers:

1. If the Gospels say that Jesus had brothers and sisters, how can Mary be called a virgin?

A. The explanation is that in Aramaic, the language spoken by Jesus, there was no word for cousin, so the cousins of Jesus were called his brothers or sisters. We know, for example, that the James and Joses mentioned in Mark 6:3 as the brothers of Jesus were in fact the sons of Mary of Clopas. Since the Gospels tell us that Mary of Clopas was the Blessed Mother's sister (John 19:25), that means that she was Jesus' aunt and that her sons were Jesus' cousins.

The perpetual virginity of Mary has been taught by the Church from the beginning. That belief is the same today as when St. Augustine in the 5th century described Mary as "a virgin who conceives, a virgin who gives birth, a virgin with child, a virgin delivered of child—a virgin ever virgin."

2. There is no mention of the Immaculate Conception in the Bible, so how do we know that Mary was conceived immaculate?

A. First of all, let us make clear what the Immaculate Conception means. It does not refer to the virginal conception of Jesus in Mary's womb through the power of the Holy Spirit. That is the doctrine of Mary's divine maternity. What the

Immaculate Conception does mean is that Mary, from the first moment of her conception in the womb of her mother, was preserved from all stain of original sin. This doctrine is implied in the greeting of the Angel Gabriel, who said to Mary, "Hail, full of grace, the Lord is with thee" (Luke 1:28). If Mary was full of grace, she was completely free from sin. Jesus gave her this special privilege because he wanted to be conceived and born of a sinless mother.

Because she was sinless and played such an important part in her Son's redemption of the world, Mary was also spared the corruption of the grave. She was taken up to heaven, body and soul, at the end of her life. This is the doctrine of the Assumption.

3. What message runs through all of the Blessed Virgin's appearances on earth?

A. Prayer, penance, and reparation for sin. She is warning us that God is displeased with the sinful state of the world and that unless we do what he asks, as related through Mary, he will punish the world. There is no greater proof that Mary is the mother of us all than the concern she has shown for her earthly children in her numerous visits to earth.

4. Are Catholics required to believe in the apparitions of the Blessed Mother?

A. Since they are private revelations, the answer is no. But the Church has painstakingly investigated these apparitions and pronounced them worthy of belief, so only a foolish and imprudent Catholic would be skeptical of these appearances. The Popes have also given their approval by traveling to these world-famous shrines. Pope Paul VI visited Fatima in 1967, and Pope John Paul II went there on May 13, 1982, exactly one year from the day he was gravely wounded in St. Peter's Square, to thank our Lady for sparing his life and again on May 13, 2000 to beatify Francisco and Jacinta.

5. Has the third secret of Fatima ever been made public?

A. During her appearance to the three children at Fatima on July 13, 1917, the Blessed Mother revealed three secrets.

Two of them—the vision of hell and devotion to her Immaculate Heart—were later made public by Lucia, one of the three visionaries. She put the third secret in a letter that was not publicly revealed until May 13, 2000, during beatification ceremonies in Fatima for the other two visionaries.

The letter referred to a bishop clothed in white who was making his way toward the cross with great effort amid the corpses of martyrs when "he too falls to the ground, apparently dead, under a burst of gunfire." Pope John Paul believed that he was that bishop and that the Blessed Mother saved his life during the assassination attempt on May 13, 1981 by guiding the bullet's path and enabling the "dying Pope" to halt "at the threshold of death."

6. How do you answer those who say that Catholics who pray the rosary are guilty of "the sheer multiplication of words" (other translations say "vain repetition") that Jesus warned against in Matthew 6:7?

A. Jesus was not talking about prayers like the rosary, but rather about "the hypocrites who love to stand and pray in synagogues or on street corners in order to be noticed" (Matthew 6:5). They just rattled off words with no thought to what they were saying. Reciting the prayers of the rosary, on the other hand, involves meditating on the joyful, sorrowful, and glorious events in the life of our Lord and his Blessed Mother.

Furthermore, repetitious prayer is not wrong or vain if it is sincere. Jesus himself repeated the same prayer over and over during his agony in the Garden of Gethsemani (Matthew 26:39, 42, 44). And Christ told us that the humble tax collector, who kept repeating, "O God, be merciful to me, a sinner," went home from the temple "justified," while the self-righteous and long-winded Pharisee did not (Luke 18:9-14).

Projects:

1. List all the feasts of the Blessed Mother that are celebrated during the year.

2. Write a summary of chapter VIII of Vatican II's *Constituion on the Church*.

3. Write a newspaper story on one of Mary's appearances.

4. Write a newspaper story on the changing of water into wine during the wedding feast at Cana.

5. Write a report on Pope John Paul's letter, *Mother of the Redeemer.*

6. Plan a "Living Rosary" procession in your school or parish. Hold it at night and have each participant stand for a bead and hold a candle.

7. Recite after each decade of the rosary the prayer requested by Our Lady of Fatima: "O my Jesus, forgive us our sins, save us from the fire of hell; lead all souls to heaven, especially those in most need of your mercy."

References:

Catechism of the Catholic Church
Daniel-Rops, Henri. *The Book of Mary*
Drummey, James J. *Catholic Replies*
Fox, Rev. Robert J. *Fatima Today*
Groeschel, Rev. Benedict, C.F.R. *A Still, Small Voice*
John Paul II, Pope. *Mother of the Redeemer*
John XXIII, Pope. *Grateful Memory*
Paul VI, Pope. *Rosaries to the Mother of Christ*
Pelletier, Joseph. *The Sun Danced at Fatima*
Vatican II. *Dogmatic Constitution on the Church* (Chapter VIII)
Walsh, William Thomas. *Our Lady of Fatima*
Werfel, Franz. *The Song of Bernadette*
Woman Clothed With the Sun, A. Edited by John J. Delaney

Chapter 23

Random Remarks on the Catholic Church

Purpose: The purpose of this chapter is to show the significant influence of the Catholic Church on world history, and to emphasize our responsibility to continue the mission of Christ in the world today, even at the risk of ridicule and persecution.

Tips for Teachers: The major task of this class is to discuss briefly some of the highlights in the history of the Catholic Church. Several good histories are recommended under references and catechists should read at least one of them. It will be helpful not only for this class but will give the teacher some background and perspective that will be useful throughout the entire course. You may be facing students who are getting a version of the history of the past 2,000 years that ignores the significant and indispensable role of the Catholic Church. Some historical knowledge of your own Church will be of benefit to you and your students.

You cannot cover much Church history in one or two classes—it should be a full-year course—so emphasize the persecutions of the Church of Christ and the incredible heroism of the millions of faithful who suffered cruel and barbaric deaths rather than renounce Jesus or his Church. There are many inspiring stories (some on videos) that can be told—from the early Christians to the English martyrs to St. Maximilian Kolbe in our own time. Share these with the class so that they can come to appreciate their glorious heritage.

The final point to be made is our duty to carry on the mission of Christ in the future. We may not have to face persecution and death in defense of our Faith, but we may have to confront something that might be harder to contend with—the ridicule and scorn of a society that has turned away from

God and does not want to be reminded of its obligations to know, love, and serve God.

It will take courage to be an apostle of Christ today—courage not unlike that of the martyrs. *Catholicism and Reason* has provided a logical and reasoned analysis of why we should follow Christ. The next step is to ask Christ for the grace to remain always close to him and to his Church, and for the courage to be a witness to both in the modern world.

Topics for Discussion:

1. Has the Catholic Church had much influence on world history? Give some examples.

2. What is the main reason the Church has survived all attempts to destroy it?

3. What is meant by the slogan, "The blood of martyrs is the seed of Christians"?

4. Will the Catholic Church ever be popular and welcomed by the world?

Some Questions and Answers:

1. Why didn't Jesus choose twelve brilliant and brave men as his Apostles instead of men who were unlearned and weak?

A. Because he wanted to show that even unlearned and weak men—with divine assistance—could convert the world. It is an object lesson to us—weak and sinful humans that we are—that with God's help we can do anything. If the twelve Apostles and their successors could convert the brutal, pagan Roman Empire, what is to prevent us from reforming our own society by living and spreading the message of Jesus Christ?

2. Did Jesus foresee that there would be Catholics who would renounce their Faith?

A. Yes. Through such parables as the weeds growing next to the wheat (Matthew 13:24-30, 36-43) and the good and bad fish caught in the net (Matthew 13:47-50), Jesus emphasized that there would be good and bad people in his kingdom until the final day, when he would welcome the good into heaven and consign the bad to hell.

3. How do you answer those who say that the Catholic Church is wealthy and should sell its treasures to help the poor and homeless?

A. First of all, the Catholic Church is not wealthy in the usual sense of the word. Yes, the Church does have a worldwide network of churches, schools, convents, monasteries, hospitals, orphanages, and homes for the aged, the troubled, and the dying. But these physical structures are not used to make anyone rich; they are used to bring the teachings and love of God to people of every nation. It costs a huge amount of money to maintain these buildings and operate the agencies and programs they house, but the Universal Church, which exists to save souls, not to make a profit, is generously supported by the faithful around the world.

Second, while the Catholic Church does own many valuable books, works of art, and historical treasures, it serves only as a depository for them. It was the Church that saved these masterpieces from barbarian invaders centuries ago, and it is the Church that preserves them today for all to enjoy.

Third, even if the Church did sell all these priceless artifacts and give the money to the poor, the proceeds would provide hardly more than a day's food to the millions of hungry people around the world. They would be hungry again the next day, but the marvelous treasures of our civilization would no longer be available to the public. And bear in mind that no one has done more for the needy of the world than the Church, thanks to the tremendous generosity of millions of faithful Catholics.

Finally, did you ever wonder why those who want the Catholic Church to sell its treasures never make the same demand of governments or museums? Is it possible that some of these critics don't really care about the poor, but attack the Church because they don't like its teaching against abortion, contraception, divorce, homosexual behavior, or some other issue?

Projects:

1. Prepare a list of half a dozen positive contributions that the Catholic Church has made to our civilization.

2. Do a report on one of the books about the persecution of the Church in Communist countries.

3. Do a report on Donald Wuerl's book, *The Forty Martyrs*.

4. Do a report on St. Maximilian Kolbe, the Polish Francisan priest who gave his life in a Nazi concentration camp in 1941 to save a fellow inmate he never knew.

References:

Carroll, Anne. *Christ the King: Lord of History*
Carroll, Warren. *The Building of Christendom*
_____. *The Founding of Christendom*
Catechism of the Catholic Church
Catholic League for Religious and Civil Rights. *Pius XII and the Holocaust*
Ciszek, Walter, S.J. *He Leadeth Me*
Clifford, John. *In the Presence of My Enemies*
Dictionary of Saints. Edited by John J. Delaney
Drummey, James J. *Catholic Replies*
Encyclopedia of Church History. Edited by Matthew Bunson
Frossard, Andre. *Forget Not Love: The Passion of Maximilian Kolbe*
Hughes, Philip. *A Popular History of the Catholic Church*
John Paul II, Pope. *Crossing the Threshold of Hope*
Kerrison, Raymond. *Bishop Walsh of Maryknoll*
Mindszenty, Jozsef Cardinal. *Memoirs.*
O'Brien, John. *Giants of the Faith.*
Rader, Rev. John S., and Fedoryka, Kateryna. *The Pope and the Holocaust*
Rigney, Harold. *Four Years in a Red Hell*
Ruffin, Bernard. *The Twelve: The Lives of the Apostles After Calvary*
Stravinskas, Rev. Peter M.J. *The Catholic Answer Book*
_____. *The Catholic Answer Book 2*
_____. *The Catholic Response*
Wuerl, Donald. *The Forty Martyrs*